OECD Studies on Water

Strengthening Shardara Multi-Purpose Water Infrastructure in Kazakhstan

OECD
BETTER POLICIES FOR BETTER LIVES

This work is published under the responsibility of the Secretary-General of the OECD. The opinions expressed and arguments employed herein do not necessarily reflect the official views of OECD member countries.

This document, as well as any data and any map included herein, are without prejudice to the status of or sovereignty over any territory, to the delimitation of international frontiers and boundaries and to the name of any territory, city or area.

Please cite this publication as:
OECD (2018), *Strengthening Shardara Multi-Purpose Water Infrastructure in Kazakhstan*, OECD Studies on Water, OECD Publishing, Paris.
http://dx.doi.org/10.1787/9789264289628-en

ISBN 978-92-64-28961-1 (print)
ISBN 978-92-64-28962-8 (PDF)

Series: OECD Studies on Water
ISSN 2224-5073 (print)
ISSN 2224-5081 (online)

Photo credits: Cover © Taro Yamada/Corbis, © Jesper Karup Pedersen.

Corrigenda to OECD publications may be found on line at: *www.oecd.org/about/publishing/corrigenda.htm*.

Foreword

This study was part of the project "Economic Aspects of Water Resource Management in EECCA Countries: Support to the Implementation of the Water Resources Management Programme in Kazakhstan". This project was implemented in 2015-16 under the Kazakhstan and OECD co-operation agreement and the OECD Country Programme for Kazakhstan developed and approved in March 2015. The project would not have been possible without the financial support of the government of Kazakhstan, the European Union and the governments of Norway and Germany, which is gratefully acknowledged.

This final report was prepared under the project to inform and facilitate the National Policy Dialogue on Water Policy in Kazakhstan conducted in co-operation with the European Union Water Initiative and facilitated by the OECD GREEN Action Task Force (former EAP Task Force) and the UN Economic Commission for Europe.

The report consists of two parts. Part I provides findings and recommendations of the study. Part II provides information about international experience with management and operation of multi-purpose water infrastructures.

The authors of this report are Dr. Jesper Karup Pedersen, Mr. Mikkel A. Kromann (both COWI) and Dr. Aditya Sood (International Water Management Institute), with inputs from Ms. Assel Kenzheakhmetova and Dr. Anatoliy Ryabtsev (both local specialists). Mr. Michael Jacobsen (COWI) provided quality assurance.

The authors are grateful to Mr. Alexander Martoussevitch (OECD/GREEN Action Task Force secretariat), who supervised this project, for useful ideas and comments.

The authors are also thankful to all within the Committee on Water Resources, *Kazvodkhoz* and *Akimat* of South Kazakhstan region. They have contributed to the project and the report by providing ideas, data and information, and various types of assistance. In particular, the authors would like to thank Yerdos Kulzhanbekov (Committee on Water Resources), Meirbek Egenov (*Kazvodkhoz*, South Kazakhstan Branch), Karl Anzelm (South Kazakhstan Hydrogeological Agency), Abdukhamid Urazkeldiev (*Yuzhvodstroi*) and Polatbaj Tastanov (*Akimat of* South Kazakhstan region) for valuable contributions to the project and the final report. The authors also thank Ms. Zhanar Mautanova and her colleagues from the Center for Water Initiatives for their support in organising the expert workshop and policy dialogue meetings at which key findings and draft recommendations were presented and discussed. They are very grateful to the participants of the aforesaid meetings for their opinions and valuable comments. Finally, they would like to thank Maria Dubois and Lupita Johanson (both OECD), as well as Mark Foss (copy-editor) and Peter Vogelpoel (typesetter) for their valuable contribution to preparing this publication.

Analysis, statements and any errors and material omissions are solely the responsibility of the authors.

This report, as well as any data and any map included herein, are without prejudice to the status of, or sovereignty over, any territory, to the delimitation of international frontiers and boundaries and to the name of any territory, city or area.

The views presented in this report are those of the authors and can in no way be taken to reflect the official opinion of the government of Kazakhstan, the European Union (EU), the governments of Norway and Germany, the OECD, or of the governments of the EU and OECD member countries.

Table of contents

Figures

Tables

Boxes

Abbreviations and terms

ADB	Asian Development Bank
AfDB	African Development Bank
Akimat	District, municipality, city or oblast (province) administration
APCC	Almaty Power Consolidated Company
ATMA	Agricultural Technology Management Agency
BaU	Business-as-usual
BHA	Syrdaria and Amudaria Basin Hydroeconomic Association
BM^3	billion cubic metres
BOAD	West African Development Bank
BVO	*Bassejnovoe Vodnoje Ob'edinenie (in Russian)*
CAPEX	Capital expenditure
CIDA	Canadian International Development Agency
CPUE	Catch per unit effort
CWR	Committee on Water Resources
EAP	Environmental Action Programme
EBRD	European Bank for Reconstruction and Development
EECCA	Eastern Europe, the Caucasus and Central Asia
EEM	*Eskom Energie Manantali*
EGP	Egyptian Pound
EIB	European Investment Bank
EPP	Electric Power Plants
EUR	Euro
EUWI	European Union Water Initiative
FADES	Arab Fund for Economic and Social Development
FOPEX	Fixed OPEX
FRL	Full Reservoir Level
GDP	Gross Domestic Product
GENI	Global Energy Network Institute

GWh	Gigawatt Hours
GWP	Global Water Partnership
HA	Hectare
HA-M	Hectare metre
HES	Hydroelectric Station
HPP	Hydropower plant
IBA	International Bird Life Agency
IBA	Important Bird Area
ICOLD	International Commission on Large Dams
IDB	Islamic Development Bank
IHCC	Interstates Hydroeconomic Coordination Commission
IMCC	Inter-Ministerial Coordination Council
INR	Indian Rupee
IPR	Intellectual property right
IWMI	International Water Management Institute
JDC	Joint Dispatch Committee
JMC	Joint Management Committee
KazSSR	Kazakh Soviet Socialist Republic
Kazvodhoz	State enterprise "Kazakh Water Management"
KfW	*Kredistanstadt fur Wiederaufbau* (German development bank)
KM	Kilometres
kWh	Kilowatt-hours
KZT	Kazakhstan Tenge
LKR	Sri Lankan Rupee
MCM, or mln. m^3	million cubic metres
Minvodkhoz	Ministry of Water Economy
ML	Megalitre
MPWI	Multi-purpose water infrastructure
MVM	*Magyar Villamos Müvek, Reszvenytarsag*
MW	Megawatt
MWh	Megawatt-hours
m^3/s	Cubic metres per second
NEC	National Electricity Corporation
NPD	National Policy Dialogue

OECD	Organisation for Economic Co-operation and Development
OIC	Ord River Cooperative
OMVS	*Organisation pour la mise en valeur du fleuve Sénégal*
OPEX	Operational expenditure
PPCR	Pilot Program for Climate Resilience
Rayon	Administrative unit of a region; also referred to as "district"
RSA	Republic of South Africa
SOGEM	*Société de gestion de l'énergie de Manantali*
TG	Turbine generator
TWh	Terawatt-hours
USD	US dollar
WHAT-IF	Water-Hydropower-Agriculture Tool for Investments and Financing, a dedicated computer-based model developed for economic assessment of MPWI
WSI	Water security index
WSS	Water supply and sanitation
WUA	Water users' association

Executive summary

Throughout the world, more than 8 000 large multi-purpose water infrastructures (MPWIs) contribute to economic development, and water, food and energy security. These structures encompass all human-made water systems, including dams, dykes, reservoirs and associated irrigation canals and water supply networks. Not only are they multi-purpose, they are also multi-stakeholder and multi-sectoral.

For MPWIs supporting irrigation, investments in water savings and agricultural economic efficiency are considered the best ways to heighten economic development and achieve greater levels of food, water and energy security. Increased agricultural economic productivity (profit per hectare) typically increases the economic productivity of water as well. This, in turn, makes it both possible and attractive for farmers to finance investments in increased water productivity.

Less certain is how to design an investment programme to develop a specific MPWI that will ensure a high economic return on investments, and be potentially bankable. Which investments to make and in which order? In 2016, a project in Kazakhstan probed this question for the **Shardara MPWI** located in Low Syr-Darya basin in South Kazakhstan and Kyzyl-Orda oblasts (provinces) of Kazakhstan.

Key findings

Water is relatively abundant compared to available suitable land. Substantial amounts of capital are needed to make unsuitable land ready for cultivation. This capital may come from farmers' own funds as their revenues will grow with increases in agricultural economic productivity (and hence economic productivity of water). In the short term, state support to investments in irrigation may be needed as Kazakhstan farmers have limited access to capital markets.

- Investments into refurbishment (lining) of Kyzylkum Canal do not pay off today, but might in the future: availability of water is quite high compared to the amount of available suitable land. Thus, additional water made available with the refurbishment is not particularly productive.
  - Severely limited future water availability might make the Kyzylkum Canal refurbishment economically attractive. The saved water will then be useful for avoiding contractions in the cultivated land area.
- Investments in increased on-farm water efficiency though drip irrigation do not pay off. The water saving from drip irrigation is quite small compared to required investment and operating costs.
  - Eventually, increased yields with drip irrigation (not studied in this project) might make investments worthwhile.

- Investments into drainage extension or restoration (e.g. clearing field drains, collector and main drains) pay off. As soil salinity is reduced and agricultural yield increases, it improves economic productivity of land. At the same time, improved crop yields lead to higher profit margins for farmers whose fields are drained.

Key recommendations

To further develop the Shardara MPWI, the government of Kazakhstan could pursue the following:

- Focus primarily on improving agricultural productivity, supplemented by water efficiency:
  - Focus investments in drainage over the next 15-30 years. This will increase profits of farmers, thereby enabling the government of Kazakhstan to increase tariffs for irrigation water and lower government subsidies to irrigation. Furthermore, it will help address the challenge of financing the water sector.
  - Gradually shift focus on increasing water efficiency through investments in refurbishment of irrigation canals and more efficient irrigation technologies (including drip irrigation) after 2030, following expected impacts of climate change on water availability.
  - Water efficiency projects may be justified before 2030, before water scarcity occurs, under two conditions. First, it could make sense if un-used or fallow land exists (or is reclaimed by refurbishing or investing in conveyance and drainage), and saved water can be used for cultivating such land. Second, it could be feasible where farmers do not receive enough water at the right time due, for example, to deteriorated infrastructure. In this case, benefits of investments in drainage are reduced since crops may wither due to lack of water. If this is the case, investments in refurbishment of irrigation canals should be launched in parallel.

Other recommendations

- Invest in rural roads, local food processing and storage facilities.
- Map the state of existing collector – and maybe conveyance – systems (e.g. with the use of drones) – and subsequently invest in improving collector-drainage systems.
- Improve statistics on agricultural productivity and water efficiency using the proposed indicators (focus depends on whether land or water is scarce, and on the situation with employment: e.g. profit per cubic metre of water, profit per irrigated hectare are relevant in case of full employment, while gross value added per cubic metre of water, gross value added per irrigated hectare are relevant in case of unemployment).

Lessons learned from 15 case studies around the world

i. The benefits generated from an MPWI typically go beyond those initially envisioned (additionally covering, for instance, flood protection, recreation and fishery).

ii. MPWI is typically associated with many positive and negative externalities: in many cases, these externalities are not limited to the country in which the MPWI is located. This calls for trans-boundary co-operation, which unfortunately is not always in place: the Lagdo Dam in Cameroon triggered a trans-boundary conflict, for example.

iii. Financing capital investment in MPWI is a big challenge. MPWI containing hydroelectric stations are easier to fund, however, as typically structures are clear for collecting tariffs for hydropower generation; these are not always well defined for water provided for irrigation. With respect to fish farming, navigation, recreation and other uses, respective water-use fees are poorly collected or do not exist at all.

Introduction

Background

This report has been prepared within the framework of the project "Strengthening the role of multi-purpose water infrastructure in ensuring the water, food and energy and ecosystems security, as well as in shifting to the inclusive green economy and sustainable development of Kazakhstan" (also referred to as "Strengthening the role of multi-purpose water infrastructure"). The project was implemented by the OECD with financial support from the government of Kazakhstan, European Union, governments of Norway and Germany, and the OECD GREEN Action Task Force (former EAP Task Force). It was implemented through the ongoing National Policy Dialogue (NPD) on water policy in Kazakhstan in co-operation with the EU Water Initiative and facilitated by the OECD and the UN Economic Commission for Europe. The text below presents an overview of the project.

Project at a glance

In January 2015, the OECD and Kazakhstan signed a co-operation agreement under which the OECD Country Programme for Kazakhstan was developed and approved in March 2015. It included an activity on "Economic aspects of water resource management in EECCA countries: Support to the implementation of the Water Resources Management Programme" (2015-16). The present project constituted a part (Activity 1) of this action, focusing on multi-purpose water infrastructure (MPWI).

It was implemented through the ongoing NPD on water policy in Kazakhstan in co-operation with the Committee on Water Resources (CWR) and the Chair of the NPD Inter-Ministerial Coordination Council (IMCC). Main beneficiaries of the project have been the Ministry of Agriculture, CWR and *Kazvodhoz*, which is the state enterprise responsible for water management in Kazakhstan and reports to CWR; CWR is subordinated to the Ministry of Agriculture. However, other government bodies in Kazakhstan (at all levels), as well as the various international financial institutions (IFIs) and donors active in Kazakhstan, may also benefit from the project.

One key objective was "to help Kazakhstan stakeholders to identify options for increasing economic and financial returns from a selected MPWI, thus reducing demand for extending water infrastructure, including the associated amount of capital investment and state support". Such options (or improvements of existing systems and water infrastructure) may affect water, food and energy security, as well as ecosystem services and flood and drought management. If that is the case, another key objective was to "show how to maximise the contribution from an MPWI to greater levels of water, food and energy security". In this way, lessons learned from the pilot case may be "replicated and implemented to other existing or planned MPWI projects in Kazakhstan".

The project consisted of four components: inception, assessment, international experience, and conclusions and recommendations.

Interim project results, as well as key findings and draft final recommendations, were presented and discussed at the 4th meeting of the NPD IMCC in Borovoye in May 2016; an expert workshop in Astana in September 2016; and the NPD Working Group meeting held in Astana in December 2016.

Purpose and organisation of the report

Part I presents key finding and recommendations from the economic assessment of Shardara MPWI:

- Chapter 1 defines MPWI, highlights typical services from an MPWI and presents the methodology applied when implementing Component 1 of the project i.e. for the economic assessment of the selected MPWI.
- Chapter 2 presents the pilot area identified (Shardara MPWI), including existing infrastructure and the final schematic.
- Chapter 3 puts forward the actions, scenarios and storylines identified, defined and simulated when assessing the Shardara MPWI using a dedicated, computer-based model. This model, the Water-Hydropower-Agriculture Tool for Investments & Financing (**WHAT-IF**), was developed within the framework of the project for economic assessment of MPWI systems.
- Chapter 4 presents findings based on data collected and model runs, followed by key recommendations of the project.

Part II provides information about international experience in managing, operating and financing MPWI systems through 15 case studies:

- Chapter 5 provides information about the methodology applied when selecting and developing the case studies as part of a limited review of international experience (Component 2 of the project).
- Chapter 6 presents the 15 selected case studies.
- Chapter 7 highlights lessons learned from the case studies.

In addition, the report contains seven annexes:

- Annex A lists all references.
- Annex B provides a glossary of key terms.
- Annex C provides an overview of institutions visited and persons met.
- Annex D contains information about the April 2016 mission to Astana, Shymkent and Shardara cities to launch data collection.
- Annex E provides information about the expert workshop in Astana, Kazakhstan, on 15-16 September 2016.
- Annex F presents the design of the model to make a solid economic assessment of Shardara MPWI and economic impacts of actions planned by key stakeholders.
- Annex G provides information about data collected.

Concrete examples

The MPWI case studies from around the world provide concrete examples of management and operations, as well as positive and negative economic, social and environmental impacts of such structures in their respective regions. The lessons learned helped better understand the situation with Shardara MPWI in Kazakhstan and identify issues to improve the economic and financial returns from it (see Part I). Lessons learned from selected case studies from different regions of the world also help to broaden perspectives while dealing with local conditions.

Part I

Economic assessment of Shardara MPWI development options

Part I presents key results of the economic assessment of Shardara MPWI development options. It identifies how economic return from the MPWI could be increased by optimising the crop mix to capital investments in lining irrigation canals and introducing more efficient irrigating technologies. Returns could also be improved by increasing storage capacity of the Shardara and Koksaray water reservoirs, reducing leakages in domestic water supply and sanitation systems or building a canal by-passing Shardara city for discharging excess water in case of catastrophic floods. The complex task of economic assessment of multi-purpose, hence multi-sectoral and multi-stakeholder, infrastructure required a dedicated methodology supported by a computer-based model and collection of hydro-economic data. Key findings and recommendations of Part I are based on analysis of the data collected and results of model runs.

Chapter 1

Methodology

This chapter defines multi-purpose water infrastructure (MPWI). It highlights the typical services provided by an MPWI such as irrigation, hydropower, flood control, drought mitigation, water supply for drinking and for industrial needs, commercial fisheries, recreational activities, and transport and navigation.

Subsequently, it presents the methodology applied for the economic assessment of the Shardara MPWI selected in consultations with key local stakeholders. This includes five tasks: define schematic; identify actions and indicators; collect and assess data; construct and simulate scenarios and storylines; and analyse results and facilitate dissemination. The chapter ends with a series of questions around potential impacts.

Purpose

This chapter defines multi-purpose water infrastructure (MPWI), highlights the typical services from an MPWI and presents the methodology applied for "assessment" of the Shardara MPWI.

MPWI

Water infrastructures are used for more than one purpose

Increasingly, water infrastructures are used for more than one purpose. Hence, the term MPWI has emerged. Although the term may be defined in different ways, this project uses a definition in an OECD publication that states that MPWI "encompasses all man-made water infrastructure, including dams, dykes, reservoirs and water distribution networks, which are used or may be used for more than one purpose" (Naughton, M. et al., 2017). Water infrastructure may be multi-purpose by design or by practice. In many cases, the water infrastructure was designed for one purpose, but eventually took on other uses.

Investment decisions are more difficult with MPWI

The multi-purpose nature of the water infrastructure has several implications. First, it makes investment decisions more difficult insofar as the impacts of an investment are multi-faceted. In the words of a recent publication on water, food and energy security:

> Investments intended to promote water security must increasingly address interrelated challenges with solutions that achieve multiple objectives … The multi-purpose nature of many water-related investments makes it important to assess the full range of risks and rewards in a given location, and to determine the most cost-effective interventions for managing multiple, often interrelated, risks; while also capitalising on opportunities for investment. (ibid.)

Typical services

Services go beyond irrigation and hydropower

While irrigation or hydropower generation constitute the most important purposes and accompanying services of most MPWIs, other services also apply. Among these are flood control, drought mitigation, water supply for drinking and for industrial needs, commercial fisheries, recreational activities, and transport and navigation. Each service has its stakeholders and economic impacts.

Economic impacts of MPWIs may be direct or indirect

The economic impacts of an MPWI and its services may be direct or indirect. A positive indirect economic impact, for example, is job creation following the development of commercial fisheries in a reservoir designed for irrigation. A negative indirect economic impact is the decrease in water for irrigation in spring and summer for farmers downstream due to construction of a hydropower plant upstream. Indirect economic impacts must be considered when preparing and assessing investment projects in relation to MPWI.

Methodology, Component 1

Computer-based model

Component 1 is focused on the economic assessment of a pilot MPWI. The consultant to the OECD envisaged a dedicated computer-based model for economic assessment of the MPWI. This would encompass its status, as well as possible actions to increase its contribution to the national and regional economy, and to greater levels of water, food and energy security.

Five tasks

The methodology applied in Component 1 consisted of five consecutive tasks. The tasks were:

- Develop schematic.
- Identify actions and indicators.
- Collect and assess data.
- Construct scenarios and storylines.
- Analyse results and facilitate dissemination.

Actions, scenarios and storylines are key for data collection and model design, analysis, and dissemination and facilitation of the policy dialogue linked with investment planning. The terms are defined below.

Task 1: Develop schematic

Aim

A schematic is used to assess and develop an appropriate model design. As a rule, the task is quite time consuming. Various data and information, including maps, must be studied and competent experts need to be consulted. This is often an iterative process.

Two issues were high on the agenda with this task: identification of existing water infrastructure and water resources, and delineation of planning zones.

Task 2: Identify actions and indicators

Aims

This task identified relevant actions to increase the contribution of the MPWI to the national and regional economy, as well as to greater levels of water, food and energy security. It also identified indicators to evaluate the actions. Relevant actions include, among others, investments. Relevant indicators are, among others, economic indicators (Figure 1.1).

Figure 1.1. **Selection of actions and indicators**

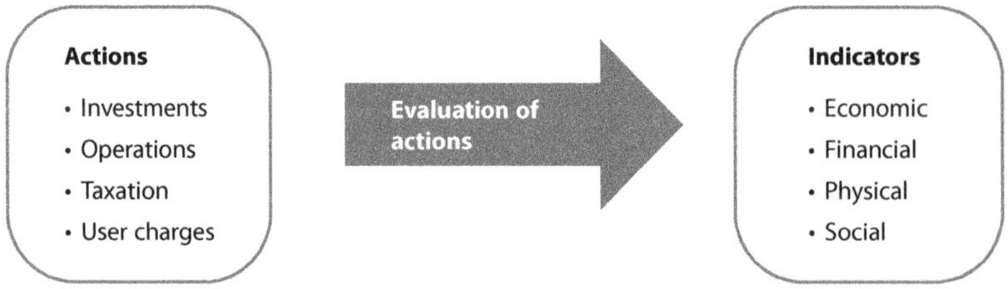

Source: Authors' own elaboration.

Actions

Actions will enhance economic and financial returns from the MPWI, as well as increase water, food and energy security through more efficient water use and improved flood management. Examples of possible actions are:

- investments in improved conveyance systems to reduce water losses
- investments in improved on-farm water application systems
- investments in reservoirs and hydropower
- investments in thermal power generation (alternative or complementary to hydropower)
- management of reservoirs for alleviating flood and drought risks
- changes in taxes or government subsidies
- irrigation water tariffs reform.

These actions can then be compared to other actions, such as no new action (or business-as-usual) or building additional large-scale water infrastructure (which implies significant capital expenditure).

Indicators

The indicators describe developments in various topics, such as economic welfare; public budget impact; water, food and energy security, including flood and drought risk management; employment and other economic benefits; and impacts on the national economy. Hence, the indicators help evaluate and compare economic impacts of various possible actions.

Examples of indicators used in the model

- economic welfare by sectors (e.g. energy and agriculture) and planning zones
- value added by sectors and planning zones
- detailed descriptions of infrastructure investment costs, including cost drivers, unit costs and total operating and capital expenditure.

Scope

The scope of the task was identification of the five-ten most important actions and indicators. More actions and indicators will make the assessment much harder to compile and disseminate. Five actions were selected for further analysis (Chapters 4 and 5).

Task 3: Collect and assess data

Aim

This task collected and assessed data relevant to the actions and indicators identified, as well as to the general entry data needs of the model.

Key task

This was the key task in that all other tasks depended on its successful outcome. As often happens, it was time consuming. Collection and assessment of data is an iterative process where the consultant depends on assistance from key local stakeholders and local specialists.

Task 4: Construct scenarios and storylines

Aim

This task constructed scenarios and storylines for analysis in Task 5. It proposed and discussed several scenarios and storylines before settling on 33 scenarios and 6 storylines (Chapters 4 and 5).

Scenario

A scenario consists of specific assumptions regarding selected actions. A simple scenario will contain one and only one action, which is compared with a "no-action" scenario (business-as-usual – BaU). In some cases, it can be attractive for scenarios to contain multiple actions – e.g. if two actions are expected to affect each other. In this case, a scenario would enable both actions. However, it is also interesting to compare with the two scenarios each containing only one single action, as well as the BaU scenario. The time horizon of a scenario must be decided upon.

Storyline

A storyline is simply a group of inter-related scenarios. Each storyline tells a specific story, highlighting certain developments, changes and impacts. The order of the scenarios is of utmost importance to the storyline.

Presentation

The scenarios and storylines were simulated in the model developed and compiled into a result spreadsheet. This sheet contains the storylines, which shows how the indicators develop with the introduction of various combinations of actions.

Figure 1.2 illustrates a storyline with eight scenarios constructed around three actions. The Y axis may concern economic welfare by sector (in KZT billion).

Figure 1.2. **Storyline with eight scenarios and three actions (example)**

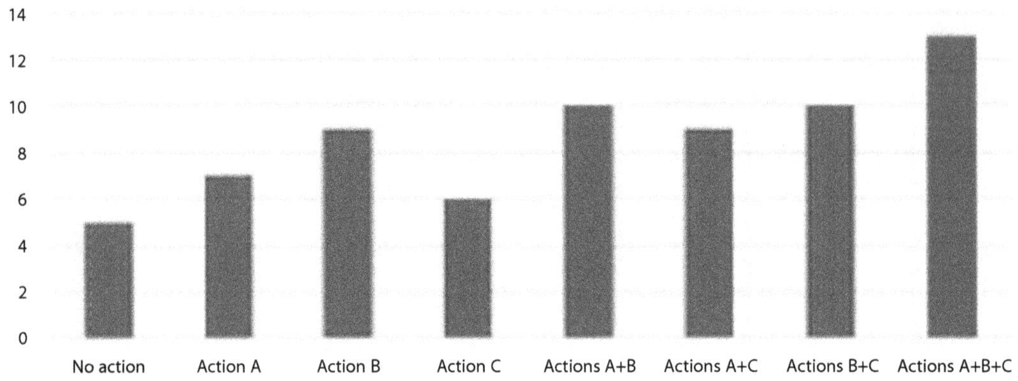

Source: Author's own elaboration.

In sum, synergies and interactions between various actions and their impacts may be presented in a comprehensive way. Changes in economic welfare, employment, agricultural output, energy production, etc. can easily be traced.

Task 5: Analyse results and facilitate dissemination

Aim

This task analysed results of the model runs and the storylines and scenarios developed, simulated and documented. Above all, it compared indicators and explained results, helping to disseminate findings and results of the assessment in Component 1.

As mentioned, six storylines were analysed, highlighting selected impacts. It implied, among other issues, finalising the model and executing model runs.

Impacts

Impacts are understood as effects of various investments and policies, especially those related to water-use efficiency, and water, food and energy security (by sectors and planning zones) on the following economic parameters, among others:

- production value
- production volume
- tax revenues and subsidy expenses
- water deliveries and losses
- water productivity in agriculture (e.g. cubic metre of water per quantity or value of crop)
- employment (agriculture only; not considering indirect employment in, for instance, food processing).

Questions

Many possible questions include the following:

- How do the costs of improved refurbishment and maintenance of conveyance canals (leading to lower losses) balance with the increased crop production coming from additionally available water? What are the other impacts?
- How do increased investments in urban water distribution systems (leading to lower losses) balance with the increased crop production coming from additionally available water? What are the other impacts?
- How do increased investments in reservoir capacity (leading to higher water consumption possibility in dry years and possibly higher energy production) balance with increased crop production in dry years coming from additionally available water? What are the other impacts?
- How does increased flood safety margins in reservoirs impact agricultural production in dry years due to lower dry year water availability? What are the other impacts?
- How does investments in collector-drainage systems improve salinity conditions and agricultural output, and how does this balance with the increased income? Which other impacts?
- What are the costs (in terms of lost agricultural output) of increasing allocations of water to nature? Other impacts?
- What are the impacts of climate change on agricultural and energy output? Other impacts?

Reference

Naughton, M., N. DeSantis and A. Martoussevitch (2017), "Managing multi-purpose water infrastructure: A review of international experience", *OECD Environment Working Papers*, No. 115, OECD Publishing, Paris. http://dx.doi.org/10.1787/bbb40768-en.

Chapter 2

Shardara Multi-Purpose Water Infrastructure (MPWI)

This chapter provides data and information about the Shardara multi-purpose water infrastructure (MPWI). It points out that the pilot area goes beyond Shardara Reservoir, encompassing water resources and infrastructure in the whole Aral-Lower Syr Darya basin. It identifies key features of the basin, such as the 80% of water flow that comes from outside Kazakhstan and its multi-faceted nature. With respect to infrastructure, it describes two reservoirs in the pilot area (Shardara and Koksaray), as well as river sections, lakes, agricultural zones, canals and drinking water. Finally, it describes the role of the schematic to define geographical areas, river sections and pieces of main infrastructure.

Purpose

This chapter provides data and information about the Shardara MPWI. It presents the pilot area identified, including existing infrastructure, and the final schematic.

2.1. Pilot area

The pilot area extends to the whole of the Aral – Lower Syr Darya basin

The Committee on Water Resources (CWR) identified the Shardara Reservoir and accompanying multi-purpose water infrastructure (MPWI) as the pilot area for this project in Q1 2016. It chose this area for the importance of the Shardara Reservoir and the whole of the Aral-Lower Syr Darya basin for the national and regional economy. The choice also reflected the extensive and complex water infrastructure in this area.

The pilot area, in this project referred to as Shardara MPWI, surpasses the Shardara Reservoir. In fact, it encompasses water resources and water infrastructure in the whole Aral-Lower Syr Darya basin. Analyses will address impacts and questions linked with areas downstream of the Shardara and also Koksaray reservoirs (see Figure 2.1). However, when it comes to actions, the report focuses on water infrastructure in and around the Shardara Reservoir, including Koksaray Reservoir.

Figure 2.1. **Aral-Lower Syr Darya Basin, including Shardara Reservoir**

Source: Author's own production based on a map provided by the Committee on Water Resources.

2.1.1. Key features

More than three-quarters of water flows from outside

As a key feature of the Aral-Lower Syr Darya basin, about 80% of the water flow comes from outside Kazakhstan. Hence, the water flow of the Syr Darya River is and will continue to be determined by natural factors of runoff formation, but also by other issues. These issues include changes in water intake, return water and mode of operation of reservoirs and irrigation systems in the neighbouring upstream countries: Kyrgyz Republic, Tajikistan and Uzbekistan.

The reservoir and basin have become more multi-faceted

As another key feature, the water infrastructure of Shardara Reservoir and the whole of the Aral-Lower Syr Darya basin have become more and more multi-faceted over the years. Originally, the Shardara Reservoir was designed for irrigation. Today, it offers various other services, most notably hydropower generation, flood control, commercial fisheries and support to livestock. In future, it will likely offer even more services, including diverse recreational activities.

2.1.2. Infrastructure

Brief information

This sub-section provides brief information about the infrastructure in the Shardara MPWI. It encompasses the Shardara Reservoir and the Lower Syr Darya River section as mentioned previously.

Reservoirs

There are two main reservoirs in the pilot area: Shardara and Koksaray.

The Shardara Reservoir, constructed in 1967, is used for irrigation of agricultural lands in South Kazakhstan and Kyzylorda regions, and hydropower. Reservoir length is 80 km and width is 25 km, and its surface area is 783 km^2. Its maximum volume is 5.2 km^3 (design storage capacity), whereas the actual volume (accounting for effects of sedimentation) is 4.7 km^3. Annual release from the reservoir is 10 km^3. Up to 1 km^3 is delivered to Kyzylkum Canal, and 1 km^3 is left as dead volume. Evaporation is measured at 850 million m^3 per annum. The head amounts to 26 m. Hydropower capacity is 100 MW. The four existing turbines are being replaced, increasing hydropower capacity to 126 MW.

The Koksaray Reservoir is located 160 km downstream of Shardara Reservoir. Built in 2011, it accumulates the surplus of winter hydropower flow from upstream countries to prevent floods. In summer, the water from Koksaray is released to support irrigation in downstream areas. The reservoir volume is 2.3 km^3 on average; design volume amounts to 3 km^3.

Furthermore, several smaller hydropower stations are in the pilot area. In Kyzylorda region, Kyzylorda and Kazalinsk hydro units facilitate operation of irrigation systems.

River sections

Syr Darya River flows from Uzbekistan are measured at Kokbulak hydropost, at the Kazakh-Uzbek border. Up to Shardara Reservoir it is regarded as Syr Darya Middle. The Keles River and canal system from Uzbekistan delivers additional inflow on the territory of Kazakhstan to Syr Darya Middle.

Downstream of the Shardara Reservoir, the river is referred to as Syr Darya Lower, which receives the inflow from Arys River. Koktobe hydropost (388 km downstream from Shardara Reservoir) serves as the "border" between South Kazakhstan and Kyzylorda regions.

Kazalinsk hydropost registers the start of the Syr Darya delta at 1 459 km below from Shardara Reservoir. The distance from Kazalinsk hydropost to the Northern Aral Sea is about 180 km.

Lakes

The water from Shardara Reservoir is released in case of emergency winter flooding and periodically during the year (upon request or approval from Uzbek side) to Arnasay lakes in Uzbekistan. The lakes emerged after the catastrophic 1969 flood when excessive water was released to the Arnasay Depression. From February 1969 to February 1970, some 21 km^3 of excessive water (amounting to about 60% of the annual runoff of Syr Darya river) was released and accumulated in the new artificial lakes.

Drainage water is often collected in artificial lakes where specific ecosystems emerge. In Kyzylorda region, such lakes include Telikul (collects up to 1 km^3 annually), Kashkansu, Bozkol bay and Makpal. Environmental flows are maintained to support some of these lakes. Kamystybas and Akshatau lake and wetland systems are regarded as part of the Syr Darya delta.

Agricultural zones

Agricultural lands associated with Lower Syr Darya are split between the two regions as follows (see also Figure 3.1):

- Kyzylorda region
  - Kazalinsk area, irrigated by Kazalinsk Canal, with a total area of 18 000 ha
  - Kyzylorda area, irrigated by Kyzylorda Canal and Aitek Canal, with a total area of 81 000 ha
  - Shieli area, irrigated by Kelintobe, Shieli and Kamystykak canals, with a total area of 47 000 ha
- South Kazakhstan region
  - Shardara area, irrigated by Kyzylkum Canal and pumping stations, with a total area of 46 000 ha.

Further, irrigated agricultural lands in South Kazakhstan region are:

- Agricultural lands associated with Arys River (Lower Syr Darya basin)

- In the ARTUR irrigation zone, Arys River flow is consumed via the canal and reservoir system; total area is 120 000 ha. Drainage water is released to Shoshkakol lake.

- Agricultural lands associated with Chirchik and Keles rivers (Middle Syr Darya basin, flow generated in Uzbekistan)
  - CHAKIR is fed with water supplied via canals from Uzbekistan; total area is 49 000 ha.
- Associated with Syr Darya Middle
  - Makhtaaral is fed mainly from Uzbekistan via Dostyk Canal; however, in water crisis situations water is also pumped from Shardara Reservoir; total area is 129 000 ha.

The agricultural zones of Lower Syr Darya are analysed within the project insofar as, for instance, investments made in and around Shardara Reservoir may affect agricultural zones of Lower Syr Darya.

Canals

Total length of the main canals in South Kazakhstan region amounts to 475 km. Total length of the extended system (main canals and canals linking irrigation zones) is 666 km.[1] By far, the Kyzylkum Canal is the most important in the region. It is 106 km long (27 km lined) with a maximum flow of capacity 200 m^3/sec. Another important canal is Dostyk interstate canal. It takes water from the Syr Darya River in Uzbekistan and delivers it to South Kazakhstan region (113 km long with a flow of 230 m^3/sec).

Total length of the main canals in Kyzylorda region is 943 km, while total length of the extended system amounts to 2 318 km. In Kyzylorda region, most canals are unlined; only 5-10% of the canals are lined.

The main canals in Kyzylorda region are the following:[2]

- The Kelintobe Canal is 88 km long with a flow of 102 m^3/sec.
- The Shieli Canal is 181 km long with a flow of 120 m^3/sec.
- Kyzylorda canal system, including the Aitek Canal, is part of the Kyzylorda hydro facilities. The left side area is irrigated from the main canal (406 km long with a flow of 226 m^3/sec). The right side area is irrigated with two branches of the canal (50 km long with a flow of 110 m^3/sec – and 78 km long with a flow of 60 m^3/sec).
- Kazalinsk Canal, which is unlined, is part of the Kazalinsk hydro facilities. The left side area is irrigated from one part of the canal (99 km long with a flow of 100 m^3/sec). The right side area is irrigated from another part of the canal (39 km long with a flow of 85 m^3/sec).

In addition, there are two old riverbeds in Kyzylorda region. These may be considered a special type of canal in that they may be used to divert water from flooding. Zhanadarya (577 km long) is situated above Kuandarya (380 km long).

Drainage and return water

The collector-drainage system is, as a rule, outdated and of poor quality. Some 25% of the vertical drainage systems of the region is in Shardara rayon (South Kazakhstan section of Syr Darya Lower), and none is repaired. Only 300 million m^3 is returned to Syr Darya from Shardara rayon out of 677 million m^3 of water used for irrigation in 2015. In South Kazakhstan regions, 724 million m^3 out of 3 km^3 used for irrigation is returned to the collector-drainage systems, and 2.5 million m^3 is returned to Syr Darya. Seepage and evaporation accounted for 631 million m^3 in 2015.

Often the water from fields is released into external collectors. The maximum level of return water in Kyzylorda region reaches only 31% of irrigation water pumped into the canal.

Drinking water

Syr Darya Lower water users include drinking and technical water supply. The main consumers are villages along Syr Darya River, Kyzylorda city (however, the transfer to groundwater source is in place), Kazalinsk town (7 000 people).

Drinking and technical water to Shardara town (30 000 people) are delivered from Shardara Reservoir (1.2 million m^3 annually).

Both regions use groundwater extensively for drinking as in general the Syr Darya water quality is not adequate to meet drinking water standards. Thus, even in the rayons (administrative units of a province [*oblast*]) adjacent to the surface water source of Syr Darya River groundwater sources are used for potable water supply, often through group water pipes.

According to a rough data assessment, some 1.7 million people in South Kazakhstan region consume groundwater for drinking and technical needs.

Fisheries

The Shardara Reservoir is also used for commercial fisheries, including fish farming; there is one fish factory. Fishing rights for individuals are under discussion.

Water intakes to serve the fishery exists throughout the Aral-Syr Darya basin.

2.2. Schematic

Top priority

Much attention has been paid to developing the schematic, which is a key element for any hydro-economic analysis and modelling of an MPWI. The schematic defines the geographical areas, river sections and pieces of main infrastructure. The analytical model can assess them and report on results.

Basis

The draft list of actions together with collected data and information on data availability form the basis for constructing the schematics. Elements not explicitly described in the schematic cannot be analysed explicitly.

Key considerations

The schematic should do the following:

- accommodate available data on irrigated agriculture in sufficient detail in terms of, for example, crop structure and irrigation techniques.
- allow for explicit description of selected key pieces of infrastructure, e.g. selected canals and reservoirs.
- allow for analysis of various diversions of water across country borders.

Figure 2.2. **Shardara MPWI, schematic**

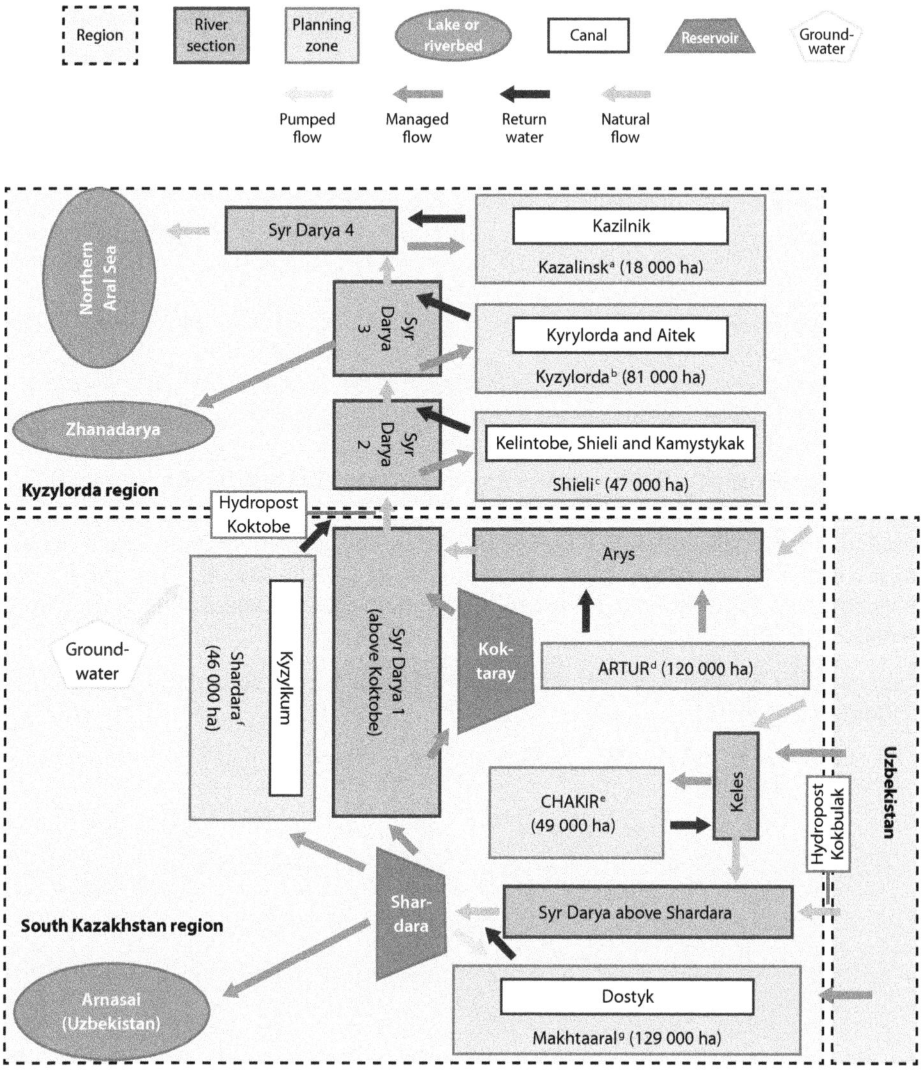

Note: **1**: Comprises Kazalinsk district; **2**: comprises Kyzylorda, Syr Darya, Zhalagash and Karmakshy districts; **3:** comprises Shieli and Zhanakorgan districts; **4**: comprises all districts in South Kazakhstan region, but Suzak district (not a part of the catchment area to Syr Darya and, hence, not included in the schematic), Shardara district (separate planning zone in the schematic), Sayragash and Kazygurt districts (separate planning zone in the schematic) Makhtaaral district (separate planning zone in the schematic) and parts of Arys and Otrar districts; **5:** comprises Sayragash and Kazygurt districts; **6:** comprises Shardara district and parts of Arys and Otrar districts; and **7**: comprises Makhtaaral district.

Source: COWI, based on data and information collected.

Planning zones

The schematic is composed of seven agricultural planning zones, three in Kyzylorda region and four in South Kazakhstan region (Figure 1.1.) The planning zones describe water use for irrigation and leaching (based on crop choice and irrigated area), as well as drinking water supply (based on urban and rural population and coverage rates). The relevant conveyance canals are attached to each planning zone for describing water losses in water conveyance.

River sections, reservoirs and groundwater use

The schematic describes seven river sections and two large reservoirs, as well as groundwater use in the Shardara planning zone. Analysis of groundwater use in other zones can be easily added to the schematic as needed.

The ARTUR planning zone covers a large and complex system of canals and reservoirs. As such, this zone can be said to be the most simplified in the schematic. Schematics will be revised accordingly if relevant opportunities for analysis arise (e.g. pumping of irrigation water) and require a more detailed description of the ARTUR zone.[3]

Notes

1. In irrigation, a main canal refers to a main distribution canal of the irrigation system. It supplies water from a river, reservoir or canal to irrigated lands by gravity flow. It has larger capacity compared to other canals. In South Kazakhstan region, the capacity of main canals varies from 200 m^3/sec to 4.5 m^3/sec (small river Sairamsu). In Kyzylorda region, the capacity of main canals varies from 226 m^3/sec to 20 m^3/sec. Please note that all data in this section are canal design data.
2. The Kamystykak Canal (30 km long with a flow of 20 m^3/sec) is not a main canal, although it is important.
3. Other comments from stakeholders, or new actions on the draft list, may also lead to minor revisions of the schematic.

Chapter 3

Actions, scenarios and storylines

This chapter lists actions to increase the contribution of the Shardara multi-purpose water infrastructure (MPWI) to the national and regional economy, as well as to greater levels of water, food and energy security in Kazakhstan. Priority actions focus on demand (drip irrigation), supply (conveyance and drainage) and risk management (Koksaray and Shardara bypass). Furthermore, it identifies eight actions left out of the quantitative analysis. It presents 15 scenarios (five actions multiplied by three types of rainfall years), comparing them to three baseline scenarios without investments. The chapter ends with six storylines (two different types for each of the three different rainfall years). The project focused on South Kazakhstan region when developing and finalising the list of actions, but considers impacts on Kyzylorda region as well.

Purpose

This chapter puts forward the list of identified actions aimed at increasing the contribution of the Shardara multi-purpose water infrastructure (MPWI) to the national and regional economy, as well as to greater levels of water, food and energy security in Kazakhstan. Furthermore, it presents the scenarios and storylines identified, defined and applied.

Focus on South Kazakhstan region with consideration for impact on Kyzylorda

The project focused on actions in South Kazakhstan region only when developing and finalising the list of actions. These actions will, however, have impacts on Kyzylorda region. These impacts have been considered in the assessment.

3.1. Actions

Investment portfolio

Actions reflect policy questions related to the investment portfolio (type, size and timing) and/or various governance actions (water pricing, land reform, energy market reform, etc.). The expert workshop in Astana in September 2016 decided the Shardara MPWI should focus on actions reflecting policy questions related to the investment portfolio.

Three types

Actions may be divided into three types:

1. demand side
2. supply side
3. risk management.

Each type may include both capital investment and "soft" measures (institutional, regulatory, research and development, etc.). In the current project, all actions are investments only. Hence, they may be presented in terms of capital expenditure.

Gross list of actions

The gross list of actions in the case of Shardara MPWI was presented at the above-mentioned expert workshop in Astana:

- Demand side (D actions):
  - D1: Invest in more efficient irrigation techniques such as drip irrigation (both better practices and investments in hardware), thereby reducing water losses in irrigation.
  - D2: Reduce water losses in municipal water supply and sanitation (WSS) systems.
  - D3: Meter water use through improved irrigation water tariff system combining fixed tariff (per hectare) and volumetric tariff (per cubic metre).
  - D4: Convert land and water use into pastures to support re-establishing and increasing meat production and processing, and leather and fur industries.

  - D5: Consider options to shift from pumping water to delivery by gravity (specific intakes must be considered; only not to Makhtaaral; demand for both water and energy will be affected).

- Supply side (S actions):
  - S1: Refurbish conveyance of Kyzylkum Canal, focusing on the whole canal or only on the unlined parts of the canal (restoration to reduce water losses).
  - S2: Invest in drainage systems.
  - S3: Reduce the length of an existing canal, while increasing water productivity.
  - S4: Consider options for increasing supply of groundwater for irrigation in certain areas (e.g. distant parts of Kyzylkum Canal) and use of solar-powered pumps. This would be important to avoid over-depletion of groundwater and maybe even address salinity problems, but may require changes in legislation.
  - S5: Adapt infrastructure to climate change (no details provided).
- Risk management (R actions):
  - R1: Provide additional flood protection capacity in the Koksaray Reservoir by increasing dam height and water storage capacity. This will allow it to intercept and accumulate more water during winter and spring floods, which may be useful for summer irrigation; the amount of winter flood depends on actions by Kyrgyzstan.
  - R2: Recharge groundwater reserves with flooding water (using excess water for re-charging groundwater reserves during flooding and then using the groundwater in dry seasons).
  - R3: Construct a flood protection canal on the right bank of Shardara Reservoir to allow excess water to bypass urban settlements downstream of the Shardara Reservoir (frequently, referred to as Variant No. 1). This investment allows some or all of the floodwater led to Arnasay lake to be directed downstream Syr Darya and possibly stored in Koksaray for later productive use.

Actions left out

In an initial review of the gross list of actions, some actions were better suited for analysis. Others would encounter significant difficulties that would render them unsuitable for analysis with Water-Hydropower-Agriculture Tool for Investments & Financing (WHAT-IF). Furthermore, stakeholders selected priority actions at the expert workshop.

Consequently, the following actions were left out of the quantitative analysis with WHAT-IF:

- D2: Reduce water losses in municipal water supply and sanitation systems.
  - Improvements in the leakage rate of the drinking water supply were not analysed because impacts on total surface water use in the basin were estimated to be negligible. Most of the drinking water is extracted from groundwater deposits not hydraulically linked to the basin's surface water.
- D3: Meter water use.
  - This action was discarded since WHAT-IF already allocates water, optimising the economically efficient use of water. Hence, water tariffs reflecting scarcity will

typically not affect the choice of crops and irrigation. If water tariffs are connected to investment and refurbishment of conveyance, on-farm water application or drainage, the impacts may be significant. However, those impacts will largely stem from the investment in infrastructure, which leads to higher productivity and hence a higher value of water. The investment and refurbishment actions are analysed in other actions described here.

- D4: Convert land and water use into pastures.
  - This action was discarded since it was methodologically difficult to make satisfying estimates of upstream economic activity (which, if needed, should have been done for producing both meat and crops).
- D5: Consider options to shift from pumping water to delivery by gravity.
  - Shifting from irrigation water pumping to gravity delivery was not analysed. Well-documented, consolidated examples of specific areas where this action is relevant proved difficult to obtain.
- S3: Reduce the length of an existing canal.
  - This action was not analysed. A proper analysis would require detailed data on yield and losses in two parts of the Shardara planning zone. These data were not readily available.
- S4: Consider options for increasing supply of groundwater for irrigation in certain areas and use of solar-powered pumps.
  - This action was not analysed. A draft estimate of the costs of increasing supply of groundwater was not favourable compared to other actions. Furthermore, the action is not well-developed and detailed.
- S5: Adapt infrastructure to climate change.
  - This action was left out due to lack of details. To some extent, however, it was embedded in the scenarios through sketched climate change scenarios (reduced water availability) and the impact of climate change on the selected actions.
- R2: Recharge groundwater reserves with flooding water.
  - This action was not considered because a draft estimate deemed groundwater pumping unfavourable.

The remaining actions were analysed with the help of WHAT-IF using the scenario and storyline structure described in Chapter 1. The short list follows:

- Drip irrigation (D1)
- Conveyance (S1)
- Drainage (S2)
- Koksaray (R1)
- Shardara bypass (R3).

3.2. Scenarios

Normal, dry and extra dry years

The scenarios depart from the short list of actions to be analysed. These actions and accompanying investments might have different benefits depending on the amount of water in each year. To account for the potential impact of climate change, all these actions are analysed for both a normal year (2012) and a dry year (2010), as well as an extra dry year.

In this extra dry year, both rainfall and runoff are 0% lower than in the dry year.[1] It thus illustrates the impacts of investments under circumstances where climate change has reduced the rainfall and runoff significantly.[2]

These 15 scenarios (five actions multiplied by three rainfall years) can then be compared to 3 baseline scenarios without the investments.

Combining actions

A scenario might contain more than one action e.g. (conveyance and drainage). By combining actions in different ways, positive and negative synergies between pairs and other combinations can be analysed with the model.

Eventually, all combined actions can be analysed. However, the number of combinations is quite large. Focusing on a few combinations is generally sufficient for adequate analysis of synergies.

Chapter 4 shows how only the economic return from drainage seems to justify the investment costs. The impact of the other actions is relatively small, and cannot justify (by themselves) their respective investments. For this reason, these actions are each combined with the drainage action. One exception is the Shardara bypass and the Koksaray enlargement. Bypassed water cannot be stored in the Shardara Reservoir; it must be stored in Koksaray. Hence, the question is whether Koksaray has the size to store the bypassed water.

Construction of 33 scenarios

The following list describes the combination of actions applied:

- Scenario A: One business-as-usual (BaU) scenario with no actions from the short list
- Scenario B: Five scenarios with one individual action in each scenario
- Scenario C: Four scenarios combining the drainage action (S2) with one of the other four actions
- Scenario D: One scenario combining the drainage action (S2) with both the Koksaray enlargement and Shardara bypass actions (R1 and R3).

These 11 scenarios with different actions enabled are repeated for the normal year, dry year and extra dry year. Hence, 33 scenarios are constructed.

3.3. Storylines

Storylines show how different actions affect use and distribution of resources

As described in Chapter 1, the storylines highlight how different actions impact on use and distribution of resources. They do so by comparing the different scenarios to each other and showing the changes. Changes may be shown in two ways, depending on which ones are highlighted:

- the change in totals for each scenario in the storyline
- the change in each of the scenarios relative to a selected scenario.

When showing changes, they are always shown relative to the first scenario in the storyline.

Six storylines analyse impact of different actions

Two different types of storylines are presented for each of the three rainfall years (normal, dry and extra dry):

- Storyline, Individual
  - All actions are compared to the BaU scenario (i.e. the A scenario and the 5 B scenarios from the list above). BaU is the first scenario.
- Storyline, Synergies
  - All actions in combination with the drainage action are compared to the drainage action (Scenario C) plus the combined drainage and Koksaray plus Shardara bypass scenario (Scenario D). Drainage is the first scenario.

These two types of storylines are calculated for the normal, dry and extra dry year.

Hence, a total of six storylines have been made, namely:

1. individual (normal)
2. individual (dry)
3. individual (extra dry)
4. synergies (normal)
5. synergies (dry)
6. synergies (extra dry).

This structure provides the opportunity to analyse whether the different actions have different impacts and synergies depending on the hydrological conditions as described by the normal, dry and extra dry year.

Notes

1. Impacts of the actions for a wet year are not reported. These are like impacts of the actions for a normal year because there is also no water shortage in a normal year.
2. This extra dry year is purely an example. Its assumptions are hypothetical and not based on any modelling of climate change.

Chapter 4

Findings and recommendations

This chapter presents findings based on data collected, as well as actions, scenarios and storylines simulated and analysed using the WHAT-IF model. It further defines five actions previously identified – drip irrigation, conveyance, drainage, Koksaray and Shardara bypass – in terms of costs and impacts on available resources. Supported by a series of graphics, it examines findings on land use and profitability, highlighting data on the source of agriculture net income and irrigation water use by planning zones, among others. It also addresses findings regarding land use and individual actions, and the synergies between them. The chapter ends with a summary of key findings and reservations followed by key recommendations of the project.

They concern the need to focus on agricultural productivity supplemented by water efficiency. Further recommendations concern improvement of water resources management in Kazakhstan in general and application of the WHAT-IF model both inside and outside the country. These revolve around improving water and agricultural productivity simultaneously; promoting investments in drainage, transport and agri-food market infrastructure; producing statistics on agricultural productivity and water efficiency; and ensuring the availability of different financing mechanisms for different types of investments. It ends with recommendations on potential applications of the WHAT-IF model, including as a pre-feasibility study tool and in strategic planning.

Purpose

This chapter presents findings based on data collected, as well as actions, scenarios and storylines simulated and analysed. Building on Chapter 3, it further defines actions in terms of costs and impacts on available resources. Consequently, it deals with findings regarding land use, and then presents findings regarding individual actions and synergies between these, respectively. All findings – and additional lessons learned, where relevant – are highlighted in separate boxes for ease of reading. The chapter ends with a summary of findings and reservations.

4.1. Actions, costs and impacts

Cost and impact of five actions on available resources

Section 3.1 identified five actions for further analysis. This section further defines them in terms of costs and impacts on available resources.

Drip irrigation

Drip irrigation was selected as a good example of efficient modern irrigation techniques. Compared to flooding irrigation, drip irrigation is assumed to reduce on-farm water losses from seepage and evaporation from 40% to 10%. Presently, drip irrigation is applied in approximately 2 300 hectares (ha) out of 46 000 ha in the Shardara planning zone. Water use of approximately 5 000 cubic metres per hectare (m^3/ha) generates annual savings of 6.3 million m^3/year. The upfront investment cost is KZT 1.33 million/ha and the operating cost is KZT 416 000/ha per year, totalling KZT 956 million/year. The total investment cost for this project is KZT 3.0 billion. With a lifetime of 15 years and a discount rate of 3%, the annualised capital cost is KZT 255 million/year, and the total annual cost amounts to KZT 1 315 million/year. The cost per cubic metre of water saved is KZT 205/m^3.

Conveyance

The refurbishment (lining) of the Kyzylkum Canal will improve the canal's efficiency from 73% to 90%. This canal transports 700 million m^3 of water per year, so refurbishment will save 119 million m^3 of water per year. The total investment costs for this project are assumed to be KZT 11 billion. With an interest rate of 3%, the annualised capital cost over 30 years (its economic lifetime) is KZT 562 million/year. The cost per cubic metre of water saved is KZT 6/m^3.

Drainage

New drainage is constructed on 15% of the irrigated area in Kyzylorda planning zone, equivalent to 12 000 ha. The upfront investment cost is KZT 123 000/ha with an operating cost of KZT 72 000/ha per year. With a lifetime of 15 years and a discount rate of 3%, the total investment cost for this project is KZT 1.5 billion. The annualised capital cost is KZT 122 million/year, and the total annual cost is KZT 978 million/year. The cost per drained hectare is KZT 572 000/ha.

Koksaray

The Koksaray Reservoir can be enlarged from 3 km^3 to 4 km^3 volume, possibly also allowing for better regulation of irrigation water during spring and summer. The main purpose of the enlargement is assumed to be flood protection. For this reason, the modelling of any additional benefits for irrigated agriculture does not account for capital costs.

Shardara bypass

The Shardara bypass allows for routing floodwater further downstream rather than discharging it into the Arnasay depression in Uzbekistan. In this way, additional winter water can be collected in the Koksaray Reservoir for summer irrigation. In the normal year (2012), the additional water volume for irrigation is 1.6 cubic kilometres (km^3); in the dry year (2010), it is 0.34 km^3. The main purpose of the bypass is assumed to be flood protection. For this reason, the modelling of any additional benefits for irrigated agriculture does not account for capital costs.

Overview

Three of the actions mentioned above (conveyance, drip irrigation and drainage) have investment costs that are mainly attributable to agriculture. The costs of the two others (bypass and Koksaray) are mostly attributable to flood protection. Table 4.1 summarises facts related to the three actions attributable to agriculture.

Table 4.1. **Key data regarding the three actions encompassing investment costs**

Category	Unit	Drip irrigation	Conveyance	Drainage
Area	ha	2 288	n.a.	11 886
Water saved	million m^3	6	129	0[2]
Unit CAPEX	KZT/ha	1 330 000	0	123 000
Unit FOPEX	KZT/ha	416 000	0	72 000
Total CAPEX	KZT million	3 043	11 006	1 462
Lifetime	Years	15	30	15
Annual CAPEX	KZT million	255	562	122
Annual OPEX	KZT million	952	0	856
Annual cost	KZT million	1 207	562	978
Unit water cost	KZT/m^3	190	4	No data
Unit land cost	KZT 1 000/ha	527 410	n.a.	82 303

Notes: 1. Koksaray enlargement and Shardara bypass are not shown in the table; it is assumed the costs of those projects are attributed to flood protection and not irrigated agriculture.

2. Return water collected by the drainage system could be re-used for irrigation. This recycling, which results in water savings, has not been considered.

3. **n.a.** stands for "not applicable".

Source: See Annex G.

The conveyance action measured in costs per cubic metre of water saved seems to be a lot cheaper (i.e. KZT 4/m^3) than trying to save water with drip irrigation (i.e. KZT 205/m^3). However, the analysis did not consider that drip irrigation, as a rule, increases land productivity. This, in turn, increases yield, thereby generating additional benefits to those from saved water; often, these additional benefits are even greater than those from saved water. Eventual increases in yield are not considered because it proved impossible to obtain solid data regarding this increase. Drainage, in contrast to drip irrigation, only increases yield and has a clear and substantial effect in this respect.

4.2. Findings on land use and profitability

Land use

Kyzylorda region's agricultural activities tend to focus on rice and, to some extent, fodder crops (Figure 4.1). Rice is virtually not produced in the districts of South Kazakhstan region. Here the districts Makhtaaral and Shardara tend to focus on cotton, while grains, fruits, vegetables and melons are more prevalent in ARTUR and CHAKIR planning zones.

Water for irrigation in the planning zones in Kyzylorda region goes almost exclusively to rice production (Figure 4.2). Rice has the highest "irrigation norm" (in cubic metre per hectare), which is many times higher than those of most other crops.

Figure 4.1. **Land use by planning zones – Kyzylorda's agriculture focuses on rice and fodder crops**

Use of irrigated land by crop (1 000 ha)

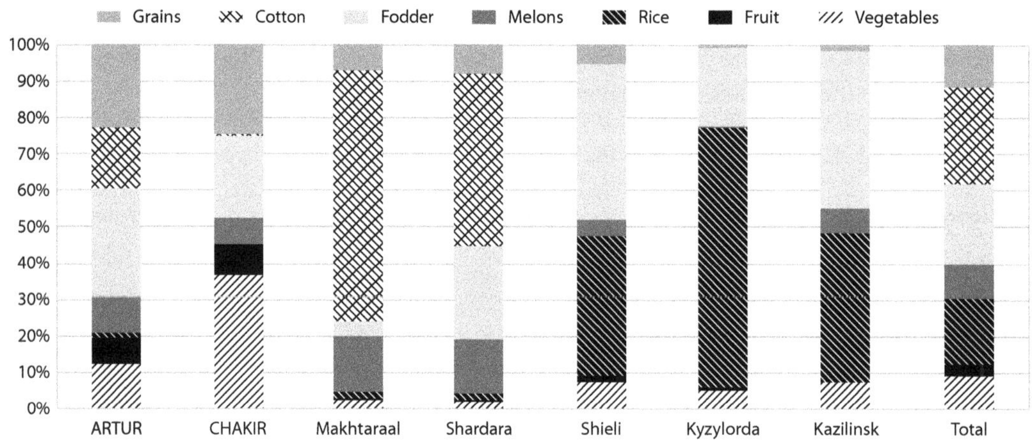

Source: Output figure produced by WHAT-IF model.

Figure 4.2. **Irrigation water use by planning zones – Kyzylorda region's irrigation use is even more focused on rice**

Irrigation requirement, mln. m^3/year

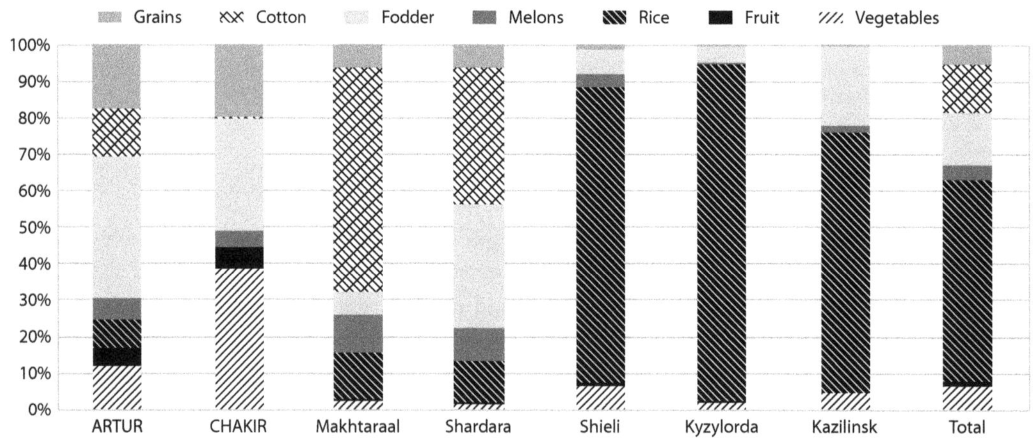

Source: Output figure produced by WHAT-IF model.

The prevalence of rice strongly contributes to consumption of 59% of total irrigation water supply in the two regions by the Kyzylorda region alone, even though it has only 30% of the irrigated area, according to the data collected.

Agricultural income

The net income from agriculture is also focused on rice in the Kyzylorda region, and fruits and vegetables in South Kazakhstan region (Figure 4.3). For rice, this is no surprise since this crop is so prevalent in Kyzylorda region. For fruits and vegetables, the high net income indicates that fruits and vegetables are among the most profitable crops when measured in term of net income per hectare. The net income is defined as crop value (*ex farm* price) minus cultivation costs (also including wages).[1] Kyzylorda region receives 41% of the combined income from agriculture in the two regions, while South Kazakhstan region receives 59%.

Figure 4.3. **Agricultural net income is mainly from rice, fruits and vegetables**

KZT mln./year

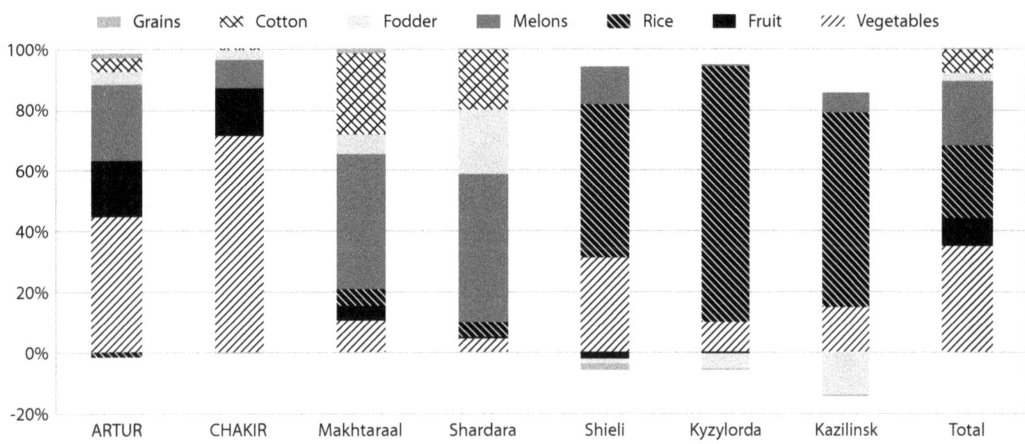

Source: Output figure produced by WHAT-IF model.

The data collected indicate that production costs for fodder crops exceed the value of these crops (in Figure 4.3, this makes fodder crops appear as a negative contribution to income). However, this assumes that production of fodder does not change between the scenarios analysed since the size of the livestock does not change. Further, some profits may be recouped in the livestock production. Therefore, the numbers do not indicate that fodder and livestock production seen together is unprofitable.

Profits by area

Vegetables, fruits, melons and rice are the most profitable crops when measuring net income in relation to the irrigated area (Figure 4.4). Melons are also somewhat profitable, while cotton, grains and fodder seem barely profitable (or even generate losses for farmers) according to data collected.

Figure 4.4. **Vegetables, fruit and rice are the most profitable crops measured per hectare**

Profit, KZT 1 000/ha

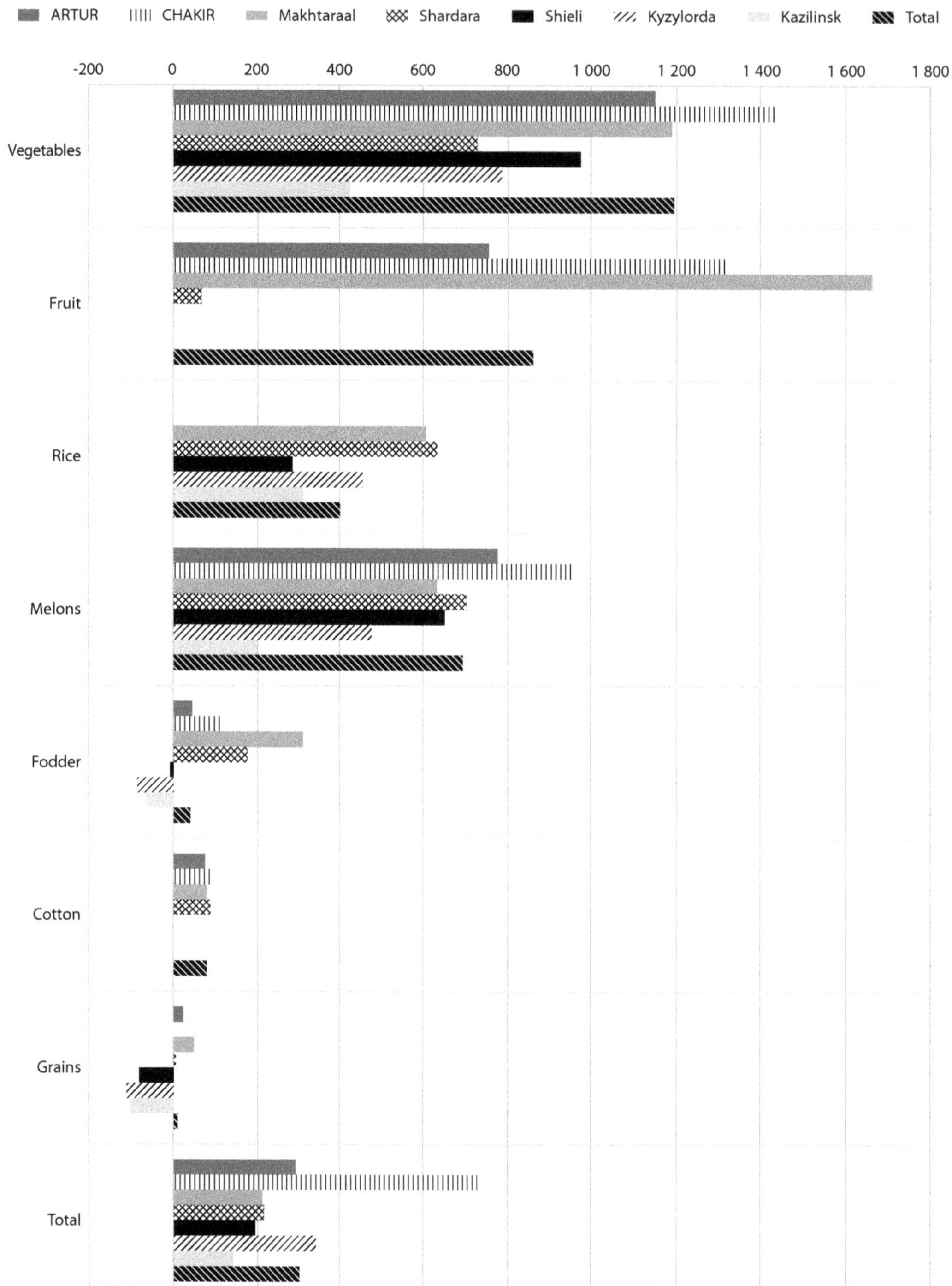

Source: Output figure produced by WHAT-IF model.

Figure 4.5. **Rice is among the least profitable crops measured by water use**

Profit, KZT/m³

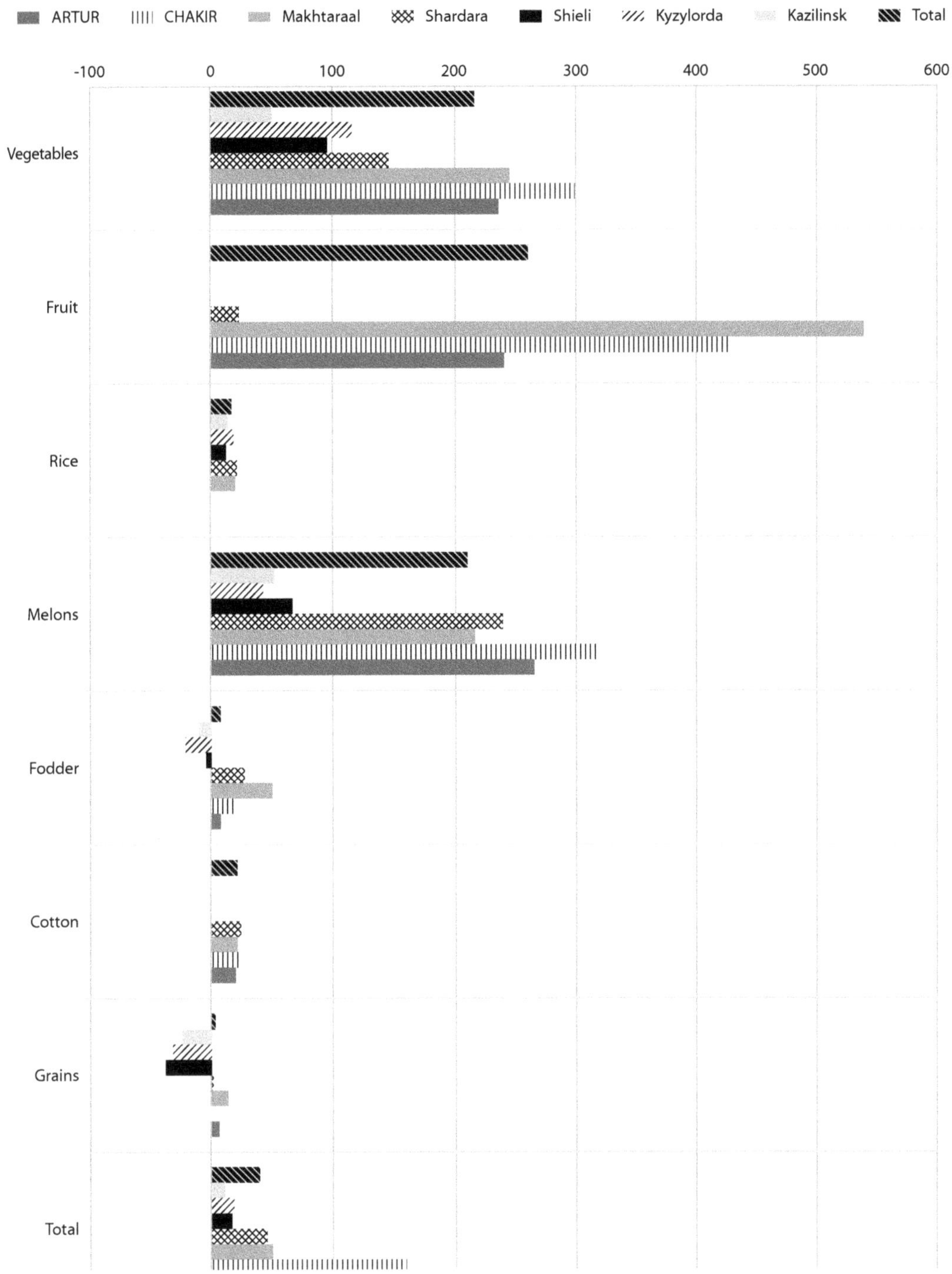

Note: The applied unit cost is prior to losses in conveyance and on-farm application. When comparing the profit per water use to the unit cost of water-saving investments, the reduced water loss should be factored into the profit per water use.

Source: Output figure produced by WHAT-IF model.

Profits by water use

Rice is among the least profitable crops when measured against use of irrigation water per cubic metre. This comes as another consequence of the relatively large irrigation norm for rice. Fruits, vegetables and melons are still the most profitable crops (Figure 4.5).

Farmers may have limited ability to shift production to less water-intensive crops

When measured per cubic metre of water used, profit can be much lower for water-intensive crops than when measured per hectar. This raises the following question: if water is in short supply, why not shift production away from thirsty crops like rice with a low net income (low value-added) per cubic metre of water used to crops such as vegetables and fruits with higher income per amount of water used? There are several – perhaps even overlapping – reasons why this shift does not occur:

- Water is not that much in short supply – in Kyzylorda oblast, at least.
- Salinity issues prevent widespread cultivation of vegetables and fruits.
- The local market is small, with long distance transport costs and related losses limiting the export of fruit and vegetables to other oblasts.

Box 4.1. **Findings on land use and profitability**

- Rice is farmed heavily in Kyzylorda, even though fruits and vegetables could raise economic agricultural productivity, both in relation to land and water use.
- When measured in relation to area used, rice is among the most profitable crops. But measured in relation to water use, rice is among the least profitable crops.
- The limiting factor for profitable agriculture is more often access to suitable land (i.e. with functioning irrigation systems) than access to water.
- Salinity issues, long transport distances and inadequate transport infrastructure may prevent Kyzylorda from increasing the share of high-value crops.

Source: Authors' findings based on the analysis in Section 4.2.

4.3. Findings on individual actions

Individual actions

The impacts of individual actions are analysed with the WHAT-IF model. The model simulates the optimal behaviour of farmers in response to changed circumstances (e.g. changed water availability due to water saving actions, or changed crop yield due to actions that increase agricultural economic productivity).

Storylines of individual actions for the different hydrological years are well suited to analyse the impacts of individual actions.

4.3.1. Changes in land use

Normal year

In the normal year, it is assumed that all available land with a well-functioning irrigation system (approximately 491 000 ha) is used. Because of this, the only action identified that affects land use is drainage. It markedly increases the possibilities for growing vegetables, which are highly profitable. Therefore, farmers use the newly drained land for vegetables. The other actions affect only the availability of water; they have no impacts on the cultivated area (or area in use). Since all land is used, the additional water made available by the other actions has no use. Instead, it is released to the Aral Sea and other lakes (Figure 4.6).

Figure 4.6. **Change in area use relative to BaU – storyline, individual (normal)**

1 000 ha, all oblasts

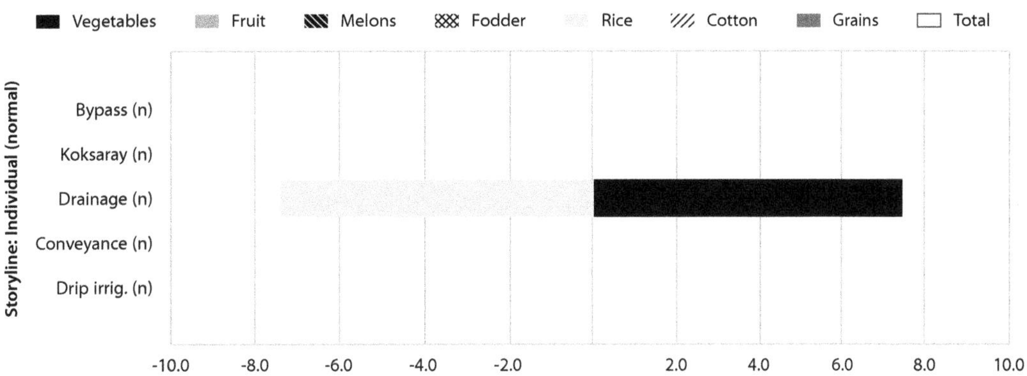

Notes: 1. Data apply only to drainage since it is the only action with an impact on the cultivated area in "Storyline, Individual (normal)" (see Section 3.3 for an overview of the storylines).

2. The letter "**n**" stands for "normal year".

Source: Calculations based on WHAT-IF model.

Dry year

In the dry year, water availability decreases relative to the normal year (roughly by 3 km³ from 25.5 km³ to around 22 km³), but all irrigated land is still used. Actions that make available additional water allow increasing the area with more water-intensive crops, such as rice.

Since all land is already used, the increase in rice cultivation means that other crops must be cultivated in a smaller area. Due to assumptions about cultivation costs and crop prices, cotton is the least profitable crop. Therefore, rice replaces cotton.

The replacement of cotton with rice happens indirectly when the various actions make more water available. Cotton in South Kazakhstan is replaced with melons, and a roughly similar area in Kyzylorda with melons is replaced with rice. In this way, local trade in crops allows switching between two large cash crops that are not grown in the same region. These changes in land use are illustrated in Figure 4.7.

Figure 4.7. **Change in area use relative to BaU – storyline, individual (dry)**

1 000 ha, all oblasts

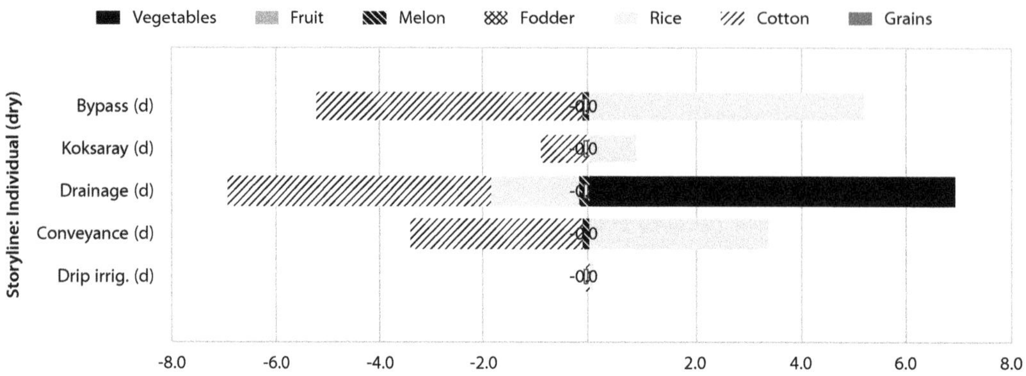

Notes: 1. Drip irrigation has no impact on the cultivated area in "Storyline, Individual (dry)".

2. The letter "**d**" stands for "dry year".

Source: Calculations based on WHAT-IF model.

Extra dry year

The extra dry year illustrates a situation with even more limited water resources, as water availability here is around 20 km^3. In this case of water scarcity, land use is reduced by approximately 35 000 ha to 456 000 ha (moving from BaU, normal year to BaU, extra dry year). The actions that increase water availability also directly increase land use (Figure 4.8).

Figure 4.8. **Change in area use relative to BaU – storyline, individual (extra dry)**

1 000 ha, all oblasts

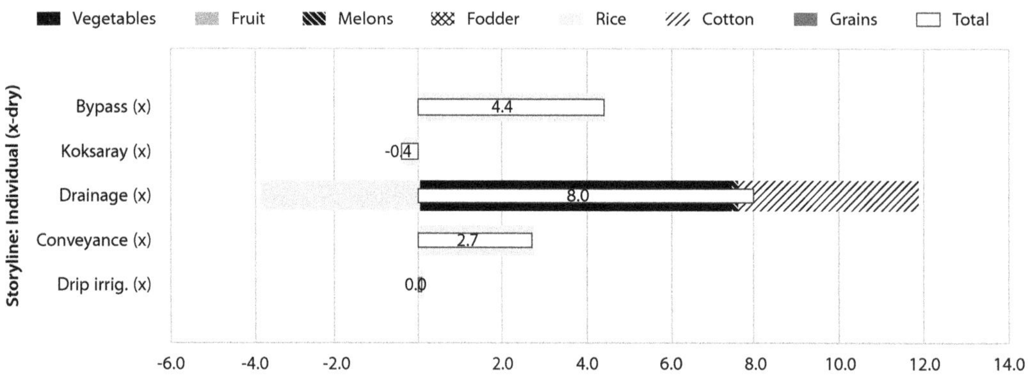

Note: The letter "**x**" stands for "extra dry year".

Source: Calculations based on WHAT-IF model.

Refurbishment of the Kyzylkum Canal allows increasing rice cultivation in Kyzylorda by 2 700 ha, while the bypassing of flood water around Shardara allows an increase of rice production of 4 400 ha. The drainage action increases the area used for cultivating vegetables in Kyzylorda at the expense of area occupied by rice. As rice is very water-intensive, this replacement frees up even more fresh water for growing cotton in South Kazakhstan.

The effect of drip irrigation is small, and the Koksaray enlargement allows a slightly more valuable use of water for hydropower from the Shardara Reservoir. This ends up slightly decreasing total land use.

Box 4.2. **Findings on individual actions**

- The water savings actions analysed have little or no effect on land use and crop choice when water is abundant and suitable irrigated land limited.
- When water is somewhat scarce, water saving actions can lead to more valuable and less water-intensive crops replacing less valuable and more water-intensive crops, as land is still a somewhat limiting factor.
- When water is so scarce that arable land is abundant, water saving actions increase land use and value created from the additionally cultivated land.

Additional lessons learned

- Trade in, and transport of, agricultural produce may allow choosing the most favourable land in one geographical location to increase production. At the same time, it allows decreased production of less favourable crops in another geographical location.

Source: Authors' findings based on the analysis in Section 4.3.1.

4.3.2. Distribution of economic surplus by agents

Normal year

Drainage comes out as a good investment in the normal year. The reason is that the reduced salinity allows growing much more profitable vegetables on the drained land. The bypass and the Koksaray enlargement have no detectable beneficial effects for irrigated agriculture. This is not surprising since water is abundantly available (relative to the amount of irrigated land) in the normal year.

Also, the extra water available due to investments in drip irrigation and the refurbished conveyance in the Kyzylkum Canal has no economic value because of the general water abundance. Hence, these actions have only costs and no benefits in the normal year. Land productivity cannot be increased more since the land is already optimally used. Saved water could arguably be used for cultivating even more land. Available data, however, suggest that suitable land is not available (see Box 4.1).

With no changes to taxation or other financing in the scenarios, the public sector bears the financial burden of the investments. The consumers and producers of agricultural goods enjoy the economic surplus of the drainage investment. This is shown in Figure 4.9.

Also, there is a small benefit in the conveyance scenario stemming from hydro power. The diminished loss in the Kyzylkum Canal allows more water to be routed through the Shardara hydropower station and to generate valuable power.

Figure 4.9. **Surplus change relative to BaU by agent type – storyline, individual (normal)**

KZT billion

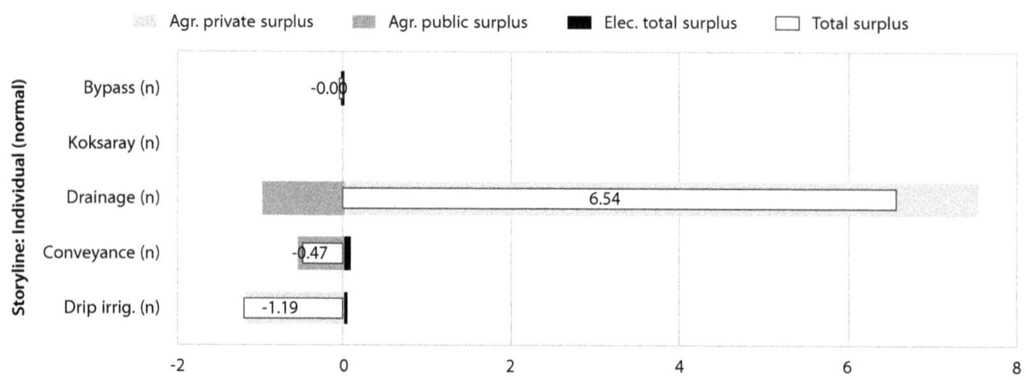

Notes: 1. "**Agriculture public surplus**" is the annuitised capital cost of the part of the investment paid or subsidised through the public budget. "**Agriculture private surplus**" is the sum of consumers' and producers' surplus from agriculture.

2. The letter "**n**" stands for "normal year".

Source: Calculations based on WHAT-IF model.

Dry year

When the same actions are analysed in a dry year, the results are roughly the same. However, the surpluses for all actions except drip irrigation are slightly higher than in the normal year. The water freed up by the investments is slightly more valuable; water is no longer abundant enough to allow full use of the most water-intensive and valuable crops. The distribution of economic surplus is shown in Figure 4.10.

Figure 4.10. **Surplus change relative to BaU by agent type – storyline, individual (dry)**

KZT billion

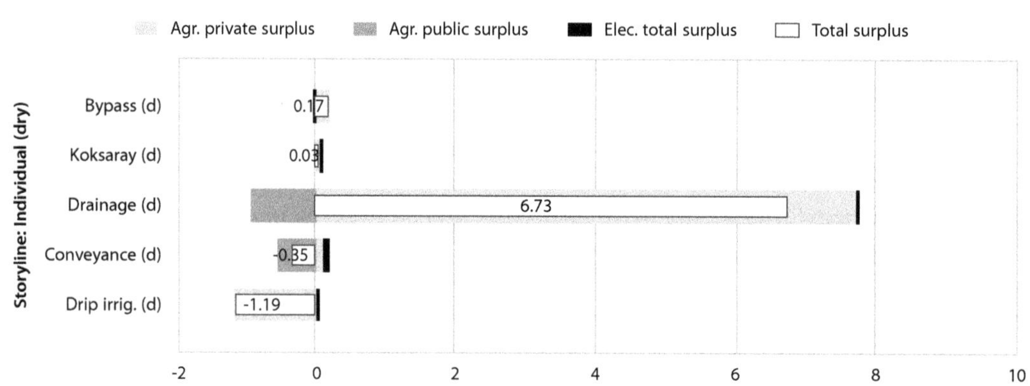

Note: The letter "**d**" stands for "dry year".

Source: Calculations based on WHAT-IF model.

Simulating the same individual actions in the extra dry year significantly magnifies effects. The bypass action has a significant benefit of some KZT 1 billion per year. This occurs although flood volumes in the extra dry year are much smaller (0.4 km³) than in the normal year (1.7 km³). The higher value of the water allows the irrigated area cultivated to increase in the dry year. The water savings from refurbishing the Kyzylkum canal are also valuable; the economic benefit from the extra land cultivated exceeds the annuitised cost of the investment (Figure 4.11).

Figure 4.11. **Surplus change relative to BaU by agent type – storyline, individual (extra dry)**

KZT billion

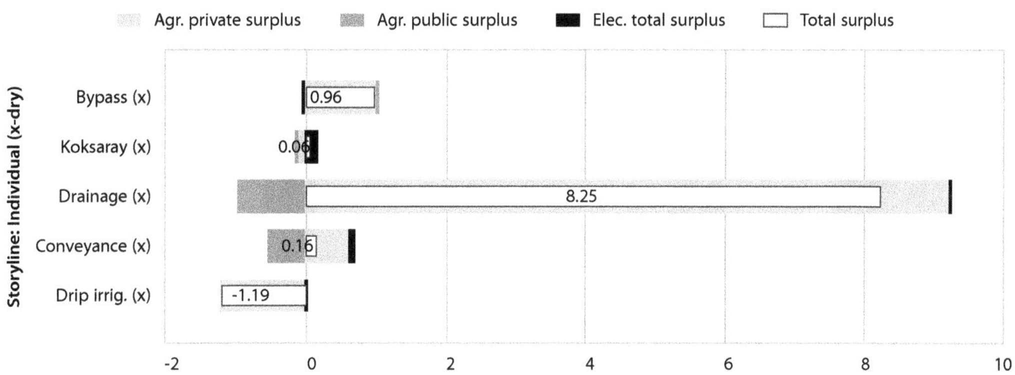

Note: The letter "**x**" stands for "extra dry year".

Source: Calculations based on WHAT-IF model.

The agricultural productivity as measured in KZT/m³ is rather low for most crops, which partly explains the meagre performance of water saving actions. As a consequence, the investment that makes additional water available must be small to recoup the investment costs. Higher agricultural productivity would thus leave more room for investment in water-saving technologies.

Box 4.3. **Findings on investments in drainage and water saving**

- Investments in drainage improve agricultural productivity significantly, and are profitable regardless of water scarcity or abundance.
- The economic value created in agriculture by saving water is smaller than the annuitised investment costs of the water-saving actions, except in the extra dry year, where water scarcity is severe.
- When water is severely scarce, economic value of additional water is high as it will allow increasing the irrigated cultivated area. The economic benefits from the additional cultivated land and water are slightly larger than the cost of investing in saving water.
- With higher agricultural productivity (e.g. higher yields due to better drainage, lower transport costs, better use of fertilisers and pesticides), the economic value of additional water would increase.

Source: Authors' findings based on the analysis in Section 4.3.2 regarding dry year and normal year.

Distribution of economic effects

Figure 4.12 offers a closer look at the difference between the BaU and the drainage scenario (see section 3.2) in the dry year with respect to distribution of economic effects both on the geographical and agent scale. The figure shows that both consumers and producers in Kyzylorda benefit from the drainage action. Producers enjoy higher yields of vegetables, and thereby better profits. Consumers gain because the increased supply of vegetables lowers the market price.

Figure 4.12. **Surplus change relative to BaU by crop, agent and region from investments in drainage (dry year)**

KZT billion

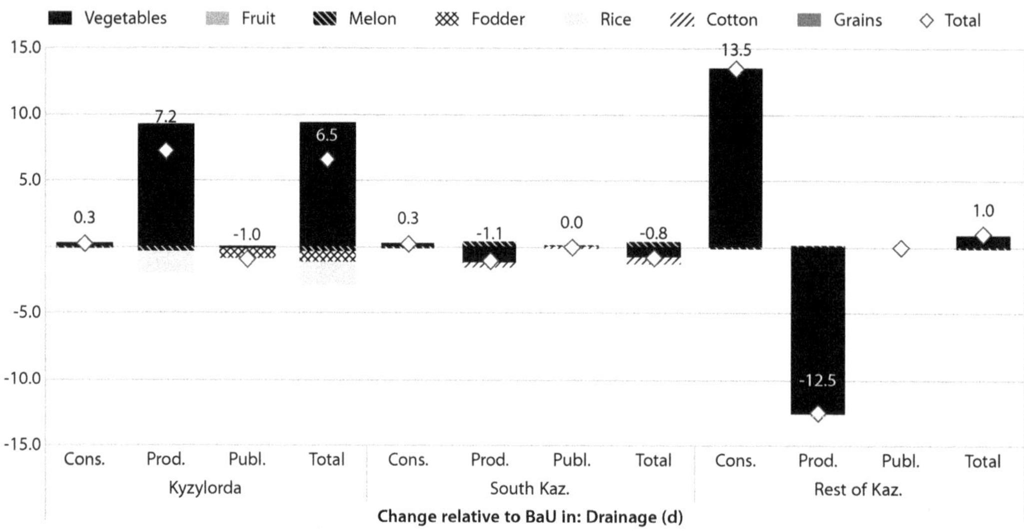

Notes: 1. "**Cons.**" stands for "Consumers", "**Prod.**" for "Producers" and "**Publ.**" for "Public".

2. The letter "**d**" stands for "dry year".

Source: Calculations based on WHAT-IF model.

Further, the producers grow less rice. This has little or no impact on consumers in Kyzylorda, however, since a large share of the rice production is exported. The price of rice is held steady by the trade with the world market.

In South Kazakhstan and rest of Kazakhstan, the picture is slightly different. The increased vegetable supply from Kyzylorda puts a small downwards pressure on the vegetable price in these markets. This benefits consumers in these markets, but it also has a negative effect on the producers.

The Shardara bypass scenario (dry year) is another interesting example of the economic effects of investments in water infrastructure (Figure 4.13). The bypass increases water availability, enabling farmers in Kyzylorda to grow more rice than without the bypass. However, in the dry year BaU, all land is used for cultivation. Therefore, some other crop must be replaced. In this scenario, melon production in Kyzylorda is replaced with rice cultivation. The lowered production of melons in Kyzylorda means that South Kazakhstan will increase its production of melons and sell them to Kyzylorda. The increase in melon production here replaces production of cotton. These effects were also described in section 4.3.2.

Figure 4.13. **Surplus change relative to BaU by crop, agent and region from investments in Shardara bypass (dry year)**

KZT billion

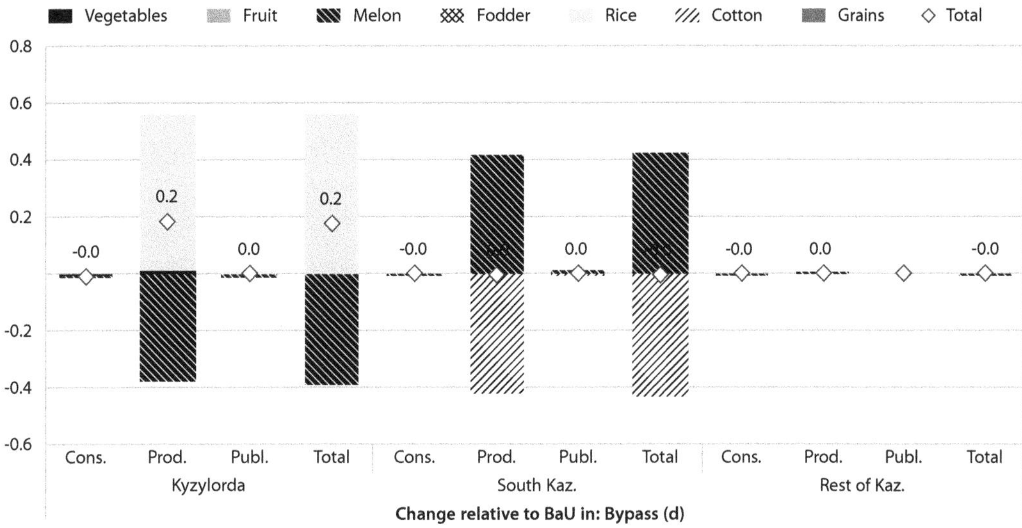

Notes: 1. "**Cons.**" = "Consumers", "**Prod.**" = "Producers" and "**Publ.**" = "Public".

2. The letter "**d**" stands for "dry year".

Source: Calculations based on WHAT-IF model.

Box 4.4. **Additional lessons learned**

- Actions that increase the output of locally consumed crops decrease the market price for that crop. If the producers' economic efficiency is unaltered (e.g. same yield and cultivation cost), these actions merely redistribute surplus (money) from producers to consumers. In other words, larger amounts of available water are likely to primarily benefit consumers rather than producers of crops (unless they are cash crops sold on the world market, like cotton, wheat and rice).
- If the actions lower cultivation cost or increase the yield, both consumers and producers can benefit. However, producers who are not benefiting from the action might have the disadvantage of lower prices and no other benefits.
- Actions that only affect producers of cash crops sold to the world market do not affect other producers or consumers.

Source: Authors' findings based on the analysis in section 4.3.2 regarding distribution of economic effects.

4.3.3. Capital costs and impact on public balances

The capital costs of the different actions are categorised by use, e.g. conveyance, on-farm equipment and reservoirs. Figure 4.14 provides an overview of the annuitised capital costs of the analysed actions. The capital costs are the same for a normal, dry or extra dry year.

Figure 4.14. **Annual capital costs by use – storyline, individual (normal)**

KZT billion/year

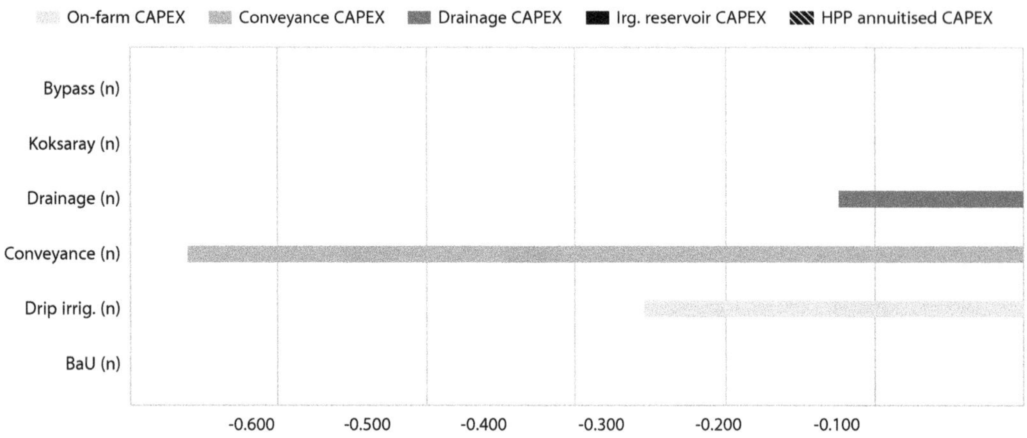

Notes: 1. "**Drip irrig**" = "Drip irrigation" and "**Irg. reservoir CAPEX**" = "Irrigation reservoir CAPEX".

2. The letter "**n**" stands for "normal year".

Source: Table 4.1.

The capital costs may be funded by different sources, e.g. directly by the farmers (e.g. on-farm equipment), or by public or farmers' contribution to Water User Associations (WUAs). It is assumed that farmers fund drip irrigation themselves, while the state funds the rest through WUAs. Figure 4.15 provides an overview of the funding of the different actions.

Figure 4.15. **Annual capital costs by funder – storyline, individual (normal)**

KZT billion/year

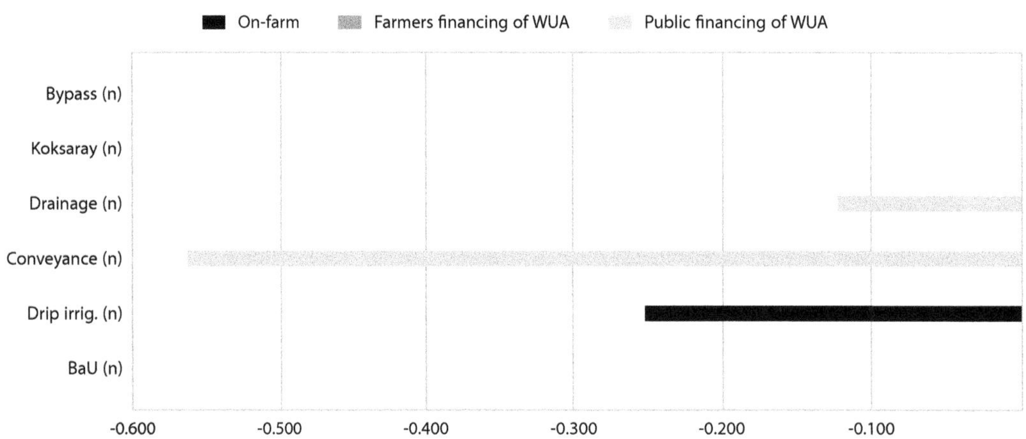

Note: The letter "**n**" stands for "normal year".

Source: Table 4.1 – and own assumptions.

The varying activity in agriculture changes the income from taxation of land and water, which are shown by scenario in Figure 4.16. The tax income is based on land and water use, which is relatively simple in administrative terms. As these resources are used to almost their fullest extent, the net income changes are of limited magnitude. The drainage action creates considerable value relative to the BaU. However, the tax income diminishes, as slightly less water is used. If taxation were partly based on the value of the produced crops, this scenario would have been likely to produce an increase in tax income.

Figure 4.16. **Public net income from taxation and subsidies – storyline, individual (normal)**

KZT billion/year

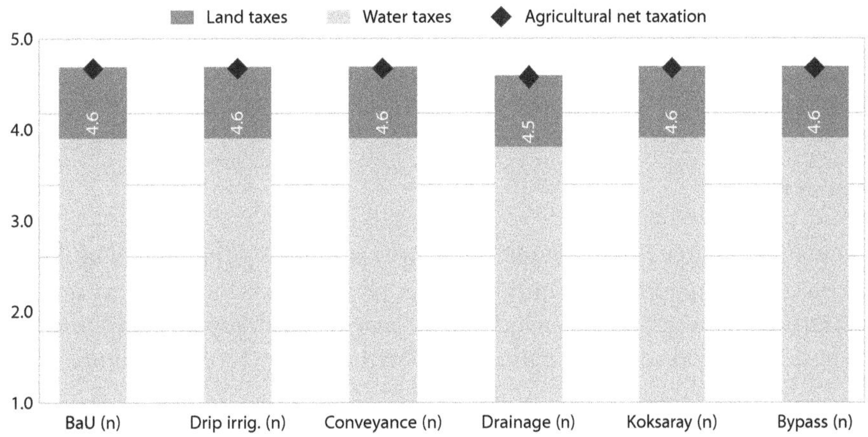

Note: The letter "**n**" stands for "normal year".

Source: Calculations based on WHAT-IF model.

Figure 4.17. **Overall public balance – storyline, individual (normal)**

KZT billion/year

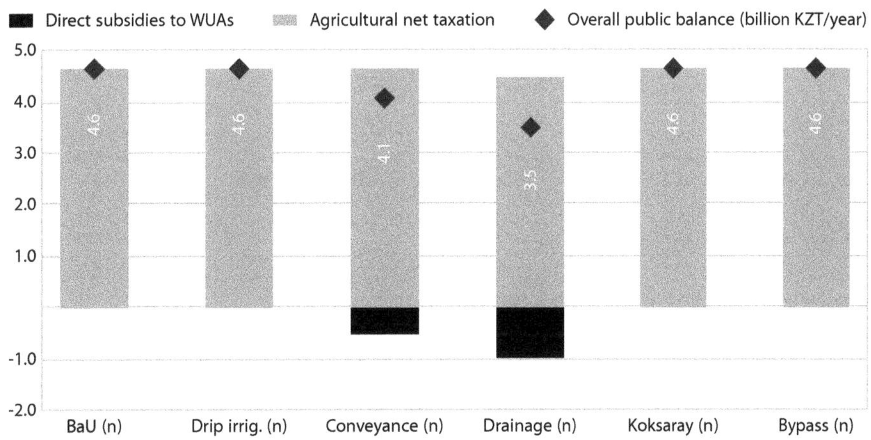

Note: The letter "**n**" stands for "normal year".

Source: Calculations based on WHAT-IF model.

The modelled overall public income and expenditure balance is composed of the net income from taxation and subsidies and expenses for funding the actions (subsidies for WUAs). The funding expenses far exceed any change in tax income. Therefore, all investments will result in a worsened public expenditure balance (Figure 4.17).

Box 4.5. **Findings on taxation**

Taxation of water and land use may be simple in administrative terms. The tax instruments struggle, however, to recoup value created by public investment in assets that increase productivity of land and water.

Source: Authors' findings based on the analysis in Section 4.3.3.

4.4. Findings on synergies

In the main finding of the individual scenario storylines, drainage is by far the most profitable investment opportunity. For this reason, all synergy storylines start with drainage, i.e. the difference between the drainage-only scenario and drainage combined with other actions. These combined action scenarios are shown for the dry year in Figure 4.18.

Figure 4.18. **Surplus change relative to the action drainage – storyline, synergies (normal)**

KZT billion

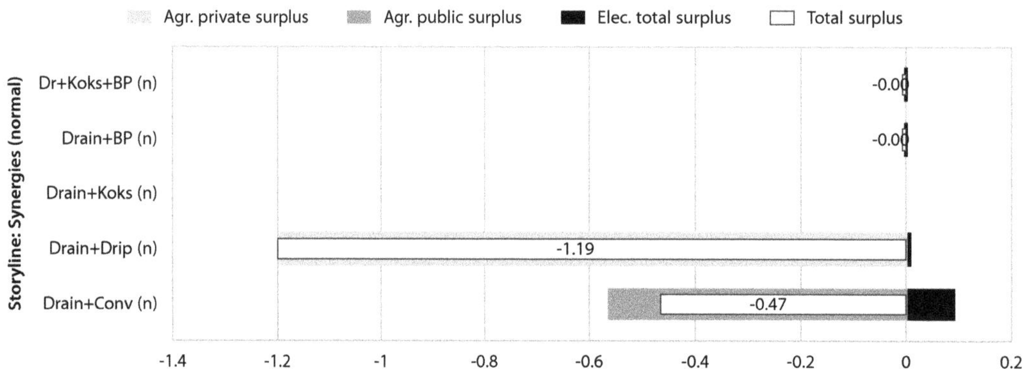

Note: The letter "**n**" stands for "normal year".

Source: Calculations based on WHAT-IF model.

Comparing Figure 4.18 with Figure 4.5 shows there are no synergies between the actions in the normal year. The conveyance and drip irrigation actions have the same outcome together with drainage action as without.

It is not surprising that synergies between drainage and increased water availability are small and/or negative. Water is already a reasonably abundant resource in the region, while high quality agricultural land is the scarce resource. It is possible to add more water even after drainage already has freed up significant amounts of water by shifting from water-intensive rice to less water-intensive vegetables. However, this merely erodes the small advantages that the actions aimed at increasing water availability may have provided.

Making the same comparison for the dry year (figure not shown) and the extra dry year (Figure 4.19) reveals roughly the same picture, where synergies are either zero, or very small and negative. Notably, the quite large gain from the Shardara bypass is reduced from KZT 0.96 billion/year to KZT 0.63 billion/year. Drainage allows converting water-intensive rice fields to less water-intensive vegetable fields, hence easing pressure on water resources.

Figure 4.19. **Surplus change relative to the action drainage – storyline, synergies (extra dry)**

KZT billion

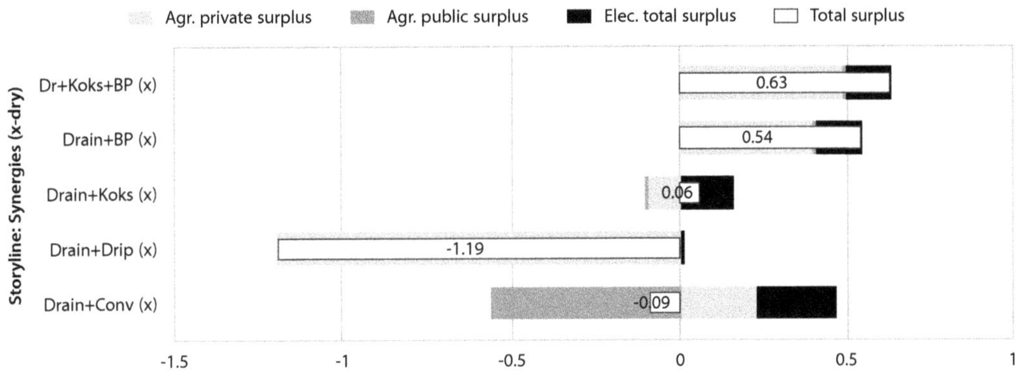

Notes: 1. "**Dr**" and "**Drain**" = "Drainage", "**Koks**" = "Koksaray", "**BP**" = "Bypass", "**Drip**" = "Drip irrigation" and "**Conv**" = "Conveyance". Furthermore, "**Agr.**" = "Agricultural" and "**Elec.**" = "Electricity".

2. The letter "**x**" stands for "extra dry year".

Source: Calculations based on WHAT-IF model.

Box 4.6. **Findings on synergies**

The synergies between water saving and drainage actions are small or non-existent. This is because drainage in the Kyzylorda context reduces water use by shifting crop production from water-intensive rice towards less water-intensive vegetables. Since water is relatively abundant, no or little additional value is created by linking water saving actions with drainage actions in Kyzylorda.

Source: Authors' findings based on the analysis in Section 4. 4.

4.5. Reservations

Important

The analyses with the WHAT-IF model – like all analyses – have their limitations. Below, reservations accompanying its limitations are highlighted so that nothing is hidden to the reader.

Data on irrigated land availability

An important reservation concerns the availability of irrigated farm land. The data received cover cultivated areas in 2010, 2012 and 2015, except for Kyzylorda oblast, where data are available only for 2015. The land available per planning zone is assumed to be the average of these three years. As the results show, water is abundantly available – relative to the amount of irrigated land – in all years except the extra dry year. If more land is available than assumed in this analysis, water would be scarcer – and, hence, more valuable – than assumed.

The land cultivation was highest in 2010, totalling 395 000 ha (South Kazakhstan oblast only). The availability was around 320 000 ha in both 2012 (normal year) and 2015 (dry year). The fall in cultivation can reflect water scarcity and/or degradation of irrigation infrastructure and land quality. Other economic factors limiting the attractiveness of farming can also affect cultivation. Since land cultivation is the same in the normal and dry year, data to some extent indicate that the fall in cultivation did not necessarily cause the water shortage.

Irrigated land in question is "suitable land", i.e. land that is economically efficient to cultivate. This means it must have a reasonably well-functioning irrigation water conveyance, and be reasonably free of salinity. There is plenty of land in the region that does not comply with these criteria. Consequently, such land can only become suitable with significant investments to refurbish water conveyance and possibly drainage systems as well. These investments are not (and should not be) included in the present analysis. Instead, the limitation on available land reflects the scarcity of capital for upgrading unused land to a quality suitable for cultivation.

Data on crops

The models' choice of crops is heavily influenced by assumptions on cultivation and soil quality, transport costs and market prices for cultivated crops. However, the modelled diversity in agricultural production is simplified with respect to crop types, yields, cultivation techniques, for example. This means that analysed impacts are somewhat stylised. Further, the most profitable crops in this analysis may not be so profitable in other situations. Results should be viewed in light of circumstances that make certain investments and crop choices optimal, and how this will impact on the socio-economy in a broader sense.

In this connection, solid data regarding the increase in yield following investments in drip irrigation were not obtained. Consequently, benefits of increased drip irrigation are underestimated; increased land productivity and, hence, yield, are not considered. Only benefits due to saved water are considered.

Model

A "one-year" model is used that does not operate with evolving and dynamic uncertainty of weather and upstream water use. This means that crop choices and water allocations are made with perfect foresight. With uncertainty to water delivery, the farmers might choose less-risky crops even if those are less profitable. Consequently, the model might underestimate the value of investments that decrease risks associated with uncertainty in water delivery.

If refurbishment of the conveyance system increases reliability of irrigation water delivery, it might contribute to increased agricultural productivity. With less risk of drought, farmers might be more willing to invest in increased productivity through more use of more productive (and eventually more expensive) inputs. Decisions on Koksaray enlargement would benefit from a multi-year model analysis.

Actions

The actions analysed here are simplified into water saving or agricultural efficiency. There are no synergies between these two benefits, but in many cases, actions within irrigated agriculture improve both. The analysis sheds light on which part of the efficiency gain would provide the most attractive improvement.

Box 4.7. **Reservations**

- Results depend very much on cultivation techniques, crop prices and the scarcity of water relative to the amount of suitable irrigated land available. These circumstances are likely to change over time. Therefore, recommendations from the analysis should be viewed in this light.
- Some limitations in modelling and data may lead to underestimating certain benefits from investments in water efficiency, especially concerning reducing the water delivery risks.
- The economic and social benefits of actions to reduce risk of catastrophic floods have been omitted from the modelling exercise, even though the benefits might be huge indeed.

Source: Authors' findings based on the analysis in Section 4.5.

4.6. Summary of findings

Actions

The following actions in Shardara MPWI, all agreed upon at the expert workshop in Astana in September 2016, have been assessed with the help of WHAT-IF:

- refurbishment of the Kyzylkum Canal to save water from avoided losses
- improved drainage in Kyzylorda to allow substantial increase in vegetable cultivation, thereby improving agricultural economic efficiency
- increased use of drip irrigation, saving water from avoided infiltration and evaporation
- additional work to increase Koksaray Reservoir capacity
- construction of a canal from Shardara Reservoir to Syr Darya, bypassing Shardara City (to be used in case of catastrophic flooding), which would allow storing more floodwater in Koksaray instead of dumping it in the Arnasay depression in Uzbekistan.

Overall findings

The combination of investments in water savings and agricultural economic efficiency is most effective in increasing the MPWI contribution towards economic development and greater levels of food, water and energy security. It is similarly the most effective approach to reducing the regions' future challenges associated with climate change. The economic productivity of irrigation water (profit per cubic metre of water) is low for many cash crops in South Kazakhstan and especially Kyzylorda oblast. This makes it difficult for farmers to finance water infrastructure that reduces gross water consumption. Investing in increasing agricultural economic productivity (profit per hectare) will also increase the economic productivity of water. This will, in turn, make it both possible and attractive for farmers to finance investments in increased water productivity.

A major determinant of the economic return on investments in water infrastructure is whether water is scarce relative to the land available. The analysis finds that water is relatively abundant compared to available suitable land in the areas in question. However, a lot of probably less suitable (not yet irrigated) land is available, but this land requires substantial amounts of capital to become suitable. In this respect, capital can also be viewed as a scarce resource.

Findings on actions

The actions have been analysed for economic payoff, impacts on water availability, and effect on related crop markets and economic agents:

- Finding 1: Investments in increased on-farm water efficiency though drip irrigation do not pay off today or in the near future.
    - The water saving from drip irrigation is quite small compared to the investment and operating cost.
    - Increased agricultural efficiency with drip irrigation (not studied here as highlighted above) might make the investment worthwhile.
- Finding 2: Investments into refurbishment (lining) of Kyzylkum Canal do not pay off, but might in future.
    - Water availability is quite high compared to the amount of available and suitable land; therefore, the water made available with the refurbishment is not particularly productive.
    - Future and severely limited water availability might make the Kyzylkum refurbishment economically attractive; the saved water will be useful for avoiding contractions in the cultivated land area.
    - Reclaiming unused irrigated land by rehabilitating or reconstructing its water infrastructure might also make the Kyzylkum refurbishment attractive; the reclaimed land can use the water saved by the refurbishment.
- Finding 3: Investments into drainage pay off today.
    - Investments in drainage improve the economic productivity of land, as soil salinity is reduced and agricultural yield increases.
    - Improved crop yields lead to higher profit margins for the farmers whose fields are drained.

- If the newly drained areas are used for crops consumed domestically, other producers of those crops will face lower prices because total supply increases. The farmers' loss is, however, exactly offset by consumers gaining from lower crop prices.
- In the mid to long term, the increased profitability of irrigated agriculture with drainage will enable farmers to pay for infrastructure costs in improved conveyance. This will be necessary to abate the effects of climate change.

• Finding 4: Flood protection investments of little importance for irrigated agriculture – today.[2]

- Since water is abundant today and thus has little economic value, the effects on irrigated agriculture from flood protection investments, such as Koksaray extension (or refurbishment of Koksaray) and Shardara bypass, are small. But, with reduced rainfall/runoff due to climate change, this may change.
- The Shardara bypass may have some merits in terms of increased income from irrigated agriculture as it provides more water for irrigation. This is mostly so in dry years, even though the floodwater amounts here are smaller (but more needed) than in the normal year.
- Value created for irrigated agriculture by the Koksaray extension may be limited as other reservoirs offer good alternatives for regulating irrigation flows.[3]

• Finding 5: Transport and agri-food market infrastructure matters – today and tomorrow.

- Transport infrastructure, transport distances and times most likely have important implications for the supply of agricultural products to the market. This, in turn, will affect profitability of water investments, although the modelling exercise itself does not document this. The same is true for local food processing and storage facilities (cold stores, refrigerated trucks, etc.).

4.7. Key recommendations

Purpose

This section presents key recommendations of the project.

Overall recommendation (Shardawa MPWI)

• Focus primarily on agricultural productivity, supplemented by water efficiency:

- Focus on increasing agricultural productivity (or economic productivity of land) through investments in drainage over the next 15-30 years. It will increase profits of farmers, thereby enabling the government of Kazakhstan to increase tariffs for irrigation water and lower subsidies to irrigation. It will also address the financing challenge faced by the water sector.[4]
- Gradually shift focus on increasing water efficiency through investments in refurbishment of irrigation canals and more efficient irrigation technologies (e.g. drip irrigation) after 2030, as impacts of climate change on water availability show up.

- Consider water-efficiency investment projects before water scarcity occurs in 2030 if un-used or fallow land exists (or is reclaimed by refurbishing or investing in conveyance and drainage), and saved water can be used for cultivating the presently un-used or fallow land.

Further recommendations

Further recommendations concern improvement of water resources management in Kazakhstan in general and application of the WHAT-IF model both inside and outside Kazakhstan:

- Improve water and agricultural productivity at the same time.
  - If refurbishment of canals is not accompanied by an increase in farmers' earnings per cubic metre of water or per hectare, it may be difficult, if not impossible, to increase water tariffs and hence lower government subsidies to irrigation any time soon, even over five to ten years.
- Promote investments in drainage, transport and agri-food market infrastructure immediately.
  - Restore the drainage system (e.g. clear field drains, collector drains and main drains).
  - Map the state of existing collector – and maybe conveyance – systems (e.g. with drones) – and subsequent investments in improving collector systems.
  - Invest in roads, local food processing and storage facilities, etc.
- Produce statistics on agricultural productivity and water efficiency using the following indicators (depending on whether land or water is scarce):
  - production/cubic metre of water, production/irrigated hectare
  - profit/cubic metre of water, profit/irrigated hectare (relevant in case of full employment)
  - gross value added/cubic metre of water, gross value added/irrigated hectare (relevant in case of unemployment).
- Ensure the Ministry of National Economy recognises that different types of investments are needed and closely interdependent, and that different financing mechanisms are available for different types of investments:
  - Example 1: a farmer finances and establishes drainage on his field (how much water received depends on the depth of main canals).
  - Example 2: *Kazvodhoz* establishes a collector canal (otherwise, the farmer's drainage system will not work). Farmers provide financing through water tariffs and the government provides subsidies, in case no private company is involved.
- Consider using WHAT-IF model as a pre-feasibility tool to identify economically sound investments and provide information about priorities and their timing:
  - It may support the State Program for Water Resources Management in Kazakhstan adopted in 2014, as well as the upcoming Agri-food Complex Development Program, which integrates the State Water Program.

- Consider the WHAT-IF model to assess implications of various financing schemes for the government budget.
- Disseminate WHAT-IF model properly to improve strategic and investment planning:
  - The model should be made available at a user-friendly website. This should have a cockpit, allowing the user to make certain choices, and to run the model without special software. It presents results in terms of selected standard tables and figures.
  - Participants should be civil servants in relevant government bodies (national and regional), researchers and PhD students, and be trained in use of the model.
- Consider applying WHAT-IF model to other MPWIs (e.g. Kapchagai, Toktogul and Upper Naryn cascade, Zambezi River basin and Yellow River Basin).
- Consider informing the Executive Committee of the International Fund for Saving the Aral Sea about the project in collaboration with the OECD.

Notes

1. Another option for calculating the net income from agriculture: prevailing price for respective crop at local market (from market prices survey by Statistical agency) minus cultivation, transportation and storage costs (also including wages).
2. Flood protection investment has other significant benefits (saved human life and economic assets) outside the agri-food sector, not linked with irrigated agricultural and value hereof.
3. The WHAT-IF model does not allow for a dynamic multi-year analysis, which could assess in finer detail the potential of the Koksaray enlargement to reduce negative consequences of droughts.
4. If farmers do not receive water at the right time, in the right amount and in the right quality due to, for instance, deteriorated infrastructure, crops may wither due to lack of water. This reduces benefits of investments in drainage. If crops do wither, investments in refurbishment should be launched in parallel.

Part II

A review of international experience with multi-purpose water infrastructure systems

Part II is divided into three chapters. Chapter 5 comprises the methodology for selecting 15 case studies of multi-purpose water infrastructure (MPWI) systems from three regions of the world (Africa; Asia; Eastern Europe, Caucasus and Central Asia) and OECD countries. Chapter 6 presents the 15 case studies, using the same template containing such elements as owners, physical characteristics, key water uses, goods and services provided, stakeholders, history, business model, key challenges, positive and negative externalities, specific regulations and the future. Chapter 7 presents overall conclusions and lessons learned.

Chapter 5

Methodology for presenting case studies

This chapter provides information on the methodology applied when selecting and developing case studies to illustrate relevant international experience and provide valuable information to key stakeholders in Kazakhstan. The 15 case studies represent three regions of the world (Africa; Asia; Eastern Europe, Caucasus and Central Asia) and OECD countries. It presents the overall criterion for selecting case studies, which concerns conditions and region. In addition, it presents specific criteria related to water supply use, physical characteristics, climatic conditions and a water security index. Tables include the final template for reporting case studies and a table of key characteristics.

This chapter provides information on the methodology applied to selecting and developing the case studies to illustrate relevant international experience and provide valuable information to key stakeholders in Kazakhstan. It also presents the final list of criteria for selection of case studies, final list of case studies and the final template to be used for reporting case studies.

Selection criteria

This section presents the final list of criteria for selection of case studies. Key stakeholders agreed that case studies should act as a set of relevant international experiences, which would inform future management practices in the case of Shardara MPWI in Kazakhstan. The key word here is "relevant".

Overall criterion

About 28 000 large multi-purpose dams and water distribution networks exist globally. Case studies should represent conditions as close as possible to those of the Shardara reservoir. At least two projects should come from Asia, Africa and the OECD regions, and five from Eastern Europe, Caucasus and Central Asia (EECCA) countries.

Specific criteria

The following specific criteria for selecting case studies were agreed upon:

- Water supply to the reservoir: The Syr Darya River, a transboundary river, supplies water for Shardara MPWI. The government of Kazakhstan does not fully control the source of water for the reservoir. This has implications on water availability in the reservoir (and hence its operations). Efforts will be made to select case studies, wherever possible, that include reservoirs with transboundary rivers as their source of water.
- Water use from the reservoir:
  - *Transboundary use:* Shardara Reservoir borders Kazakhstan and Uzbekistan. The two countries share water from the reservoir, making it a transboundary water-use system. Efforts will be made to include case studies with similar situations, but it may be difficult to find information about 15-20 of such cases.
  - *Water users:* Water from Shardara Reservoir is predominantly used for hydropower generation and irrigation. It also protects against floods. Case studies with similar water uses will be selected.
- Physical characteristics:
  - *Surface area and storage capacity*: Reservoirs selected will be similar in size to Shardara reservoir.
  - *Degree of (reservoir) regulation*: This is defined as the ratio between storage capacity and water inflow. The selected reservoirs will have a degree of regulation comparable to that of Shardara Reservoir.
- Climatic conditions: Reservoirs in a climatic zone similar to Shardara Reservoir will be selected as case studies.

- Water security index: Water supply and demand depend upon the availability of water resources and population within a region. A simple water security index – per capita water availability – will be used as a criterion to filter out reservoirs that are not like Shardara reservoir. If it is not possible to meet this criterion in some regions, it will be ignored.

Template

A template for presenting case studies (see Table 5.1) was developed and agreed upon with stakeholders (see Annex D).

Table 5.1. **Template, case studies**

Flag of country	Map 1 (e.g. region in the country)	Map 2
Owners, including asset ownership		
Physical characteristics (volume, surface area, residence time, etc.)		
Key water uses: Irrigation, hydropower, flood and drought risk management, others		
Goods and services provided		
Stakeholders		
Brief history		
Business model for MPWI financing, including cost recovery		
Key challenges		
Positive externalities		
Negative externalities		
Specific regulations		
Plans		
References (sources of information)		

Source: Own elaboration by COWI and IWMI.

Candidate case studies

A list of candidate case studies was prepared based on selection criteria (see Table 5.2). The case studies are all like Shardara MPWI in terms of the source of water (transboundary river), physical characteristics (storage capacity, etc.), climatic conditions (including water stress index) and the mix of water uses. They were reported upon using the above template (see Table 5.1).

Table 5.2. **Case studies, key characteristics**

Reservoir name	Dam name	Country	Region	River	Basin	Upstream countries	Area (km^2)	Water use (main)	Water use (minor)	Climatic condition	WSI (m^3/inhab/year)
Hendrik Lake	Hendrik Verwoerd, Gariep	South Africa	Africa	Orange	Orange	Lesotho	294.3	Irrigation	Hydropower	Arid	1 007
Jebel Lake	Jebel Aulia	Sudan	Africa	White Nile	Nile	South Sudan, Uganda	933.4	Irrigation	Hydropower, Fisheries	Arid	1 560
Lake Lagdo	Lagdo	Cameroon	Africa	Benoue	Niger	N/A	622.6	Irrigation	Hydropower	Tropical Wet & Dry	14 957
Manantali Lake	Manantali	Mali	Africa	Bafing	Senegal	Guinea	438.4	Irrigation	Hydropower, Fisheries	Semi-arid	7 870
Lake Assad	Tabqa	Syria	Asia	Euphrates	Tigris Euphrates	Turkey	636.8	Irrigation	Hydropower	Arid	791.4
Gandhi Sagar	Gandhi Sagar	India	Asia	Chambal	Chambal	N/A	523.5/ 723	Irrigation	Hydropower	Semi-arid	1 103
Hirakud Lake	Hirakud	India	Asia	Mahanadi	Brahmari	N/A	500.7	Irrigation	Hydropower, Flood control	Tropical Wet	1 618
Doosti Reservoir	Iran-Turkmenistan Friendship Dam	Turkmenistan	EECCA	Harirud	N/A	Afghanistan	30	Irrigation	Drinking water, Hydropower	Arid	4 901
Kapchagay	Kapchagay	Kazakhstan	EECCA	Ili	Yili_He	China	1 206	Irrigation, hydropower	Fisheries	Semi-arid	7 061
Bakhri Tojik	Kayrakkum	Tajikistan	EECCA	Syr-Daria	Amudarja	Kyrgyzstan	429.9	Hydroelectricity, irrigation	Ramsar Site	Semi-arid	2 338
Nurek	Nurek	Tajikistan	EECCA	Vakhsh	Amudarja	Kyrgyzstan	62	Irrigation	Hydropower	Arid	2 338
Toktogul	Toktogul	Kyrgyzstan	EECCA	Naryn	Syrdarja	N/A	223.5	Hydropower	Irrigation	Arid	4 263
Lake Tisza	Tisza	Hungary	EU/OECD	Tisza	Danube	Slovakia	119	Flood control	Tourism	Humid Subtropical	10 388
Lake Argyle	Ord River	Australia	OECD	Ord	Central Australia	N/A	829.2	Irrigation	Ramsar Wetland/ Conservation	Tropical Wet & Dry	23 346
Lake Mead	Hoover Dam	United States	OECD	Colorado	Colorado	N/A	571	Flood control	Irrigation	Arid	8 758

Source: Own elaboration by COWI and IWMI based on information and data included in Chapter 6.

Chapter 6

Case studies

Chapter 6 presents the 15 case studies, using the same template containing such elements as owners, physical characteristics, key water uses, goods and services provided, stakeholders, history, business model, key challenges, positive and negative externalities, specific regulations and the future. The case studies, which were selected according to specific criteria, represent three regions of the world (Africa; Asia; Eastern Europe, Caucasus and Central Asia) and OECD countries. The countries represented are the Republic of South Africa, Sudan, Cameroon, Mali, Syria, India, Iran-Turkmenistan, Tajikistan, Kazakhstan, Kyrgyzstan, Hungary, Australia and the United States.

Purpose

This chapter presents details of the final list of 15 case studies. They were selected according to specific criteria and based on a template explained in the previous section. The case studies represent three regions of the world plus the OECD (see Table 6.1 and Figure 6.1).

Table 6.1. **Case studies, overview**

Region	MWPI
Africa	Gariep Dam, Orange River Basin, Republic of South Africa (RSA) Jebel Aulia, White Nile River Basin, Sudan Lake Lagdo, Benue River Basin, Cameroon Lake Manantali, Senegal River Basin, Mali
Asia	Lake Assad (Tabqa Dam), Euphrates River Basin, Syria Gandhi Sagar, Chambal River Basin, Madhya Pradesh, India Hirakud Lake, Mahanadi River Basin, India
EECCA	Iran-Turkmenistan Friendship Dam/Doosti Reservoir), Harirud border river between Iran and Turkmenistan Kapchagay Reservoir, Ili River (Lake Balkhash Basin), Kazhakstan Kayakkum Reservoir, Syr-Darya River Basin (Aral Sea Basin), Tajikistan Nurek Reservoir, Vakhsh River (Aral Sea Basin), Tajikistan Toktogul Reservoir, Naryn River (Syr-Darya, Aral Sea Basin), Kyrgyzstan
OECD	Lake Tisza (Kisköre Reservoir), Tisza River (Danube Basin), Hungary Lake Argyle, Ord River Basin, Australia Lake Mead (Hoover Dam), Colorado River Basin, United States of America

Source: Own elaboration by COWI and IWMI.

Figure 6.1. **Case study, overview**

Source: the map was developed by IWMI using Arc and GRandD database.

6.1. Gariep Dam, Orange River Basin, Republic of South Africa (RSA)

Owners, including asset ownership

- Department of Water Affairs, Republic of South Africa
- ESKOM Company (national electricity supplier) is responsible for hydroelectricity production.

Physical characteristics

- Volume: 5 673.8 MCM
- Surface area: 249.3 km^2
- Residence time: 120.5%
- Total internal renewable water resources per capita: 822 m^3/inhabitant/year
- Climatic condition: Arid
- Transboundary users: Not applicable
- Largest dam and a major tourist destination in South Africa – up to 200 000 visitors a year (World Commission on Dams, 2000a; Wikipedia, 2016a).

Key water uses

Irrigation, hydropower generation, domestic and industrial use.

Irrigation

Gariep Dam plays a major role in irrigation development in the middle and lower Orange River Basin, through regulation of river flow between Gariep and Vanderkloof dams. The Orange-Fish tunnel (82.8 km) extends from the Gariep Dam and directs water to the Great Fish River to provide water to the Eastern Cape region (Anon, 2016b).

The irrigated area of the Gariep and Vanderkloof dams is 138 000-164 000 ha (World Commission on Dams, 2000a).

Hydropower

With a flow rate of 800 m^3/s, the four generators (90 MW each) of the dam's hydroelectric station have a total capacity of generating 360 MW.

Flood and drought risk management

The dams on the Orange River constructed under the Orange River Development Project are focused on reducing the flood incidence by 50% (World Commission on Dams, 2000b).

Others

Orange River Development Project provides 0.37 MCM of water per day for municipal water supply (World Commission on Dams, 2000b).

Goods and services provided

Hydroelectricity, irrigation, fisheries, tourism and recreation, drinking water supply.

Stakeholders

Government

- Government of South Africa
- Department of Water Affairs
- ESKOM.

Primary users

- Farmers
- Farm workers
- Livestock producers
- Households (drinking water and electricity users).

Others

- Tourists
- Tourism industries
- Research institutes
- Fishers.

Brief history

The potential of water storage in the Orange River has been discussed since the 1870s. In 1912, Dr. Alfred Lewis, a director in the Department of Irrigation, wrote a report on his exploration of the Orange River. This report was used to plan the Orange River Development Project. It suggested diverting the Orange River to Great Fish and Sundays Rivers through a tunnel. Initial planning focused on providing water from the "wet" east for irrigation in the "dry" middle and lower Orange River regions. The project was politically motivated and designed in haste. This led to multiple revisions of the design and an increase in the cost of the project.

In 1944, a technical report led to field surveys and drilling. The government subsequently proposed a dam on the Orange River to store and divert water to the Great Fish River Valley. Due to the government's economic constraints, it did not start building the dam until 1966. It awarded the main construction contract to the French-South African consortium of Union Corporation-Dumez-Borie Dams. The entire project was to be completed in six phases over 30 years. In September 1971, Gariep Dam started storing water and was commissioned. As part of the Orange River Development Project, another dam – Vanderkloof Dam – was built downstream in 1977 to generate hydropower; the Gariep Dam controls water from Vanderkloof Dam (Anon, 2016a).

Business model for MPWI financing, including cost recovery

The project cost was USD 571 million (1998 prices).

The South African side of the consortium was responsible for labour and management, general engineering services, office facilities, and secretarial and medical-related activities. France supplied specialist engineers.

There has been no intention to recover capital costs of the development project. However, irrigation charges have been increased to cover operational costs. The initial rate for agricultural water use was 4% of gross income per morgen of land (about R12/morgen). However, initial analysis showed it should be more than R502/morgen (1 morgen equals approximately 0.2 to 1 ha). In 1984-85, the upper limit for agricultural water-use rates was announced, which led to collection at a rate of R76/ha (based on the 1993 agricultural census). According to the 1999 agricultural census, the rate covered nearly 80% of operating costs.

In the case of electricity generation, ESKOM pays the Department of Water Affairs a fixed monthly tariff of 40 cents per kW of installed capacity. It also pays a fixed amount of 0.125 cents per kWh of electrical power generation distributed to the national grid (World Commission on Dams, 2000b).

Key challenges

- No ecological studies were undertaken: due to lack of detailed baseline data on biological habitats before construction of the dam, it is not possible to quantify or identify the dam's environmental impact.
- Irrigation target not fully achieved: only 68% of the projected irrigated areas of the Orange River Development Project has been achieved.
- Water supply target not achieved: as of 1994, the project had only met 16% of its expected final target in the context of inter-basin transfers for municipal and industrial water supply to the Fish-Sundays Basin.
- Sedimentation in the reservoir and related water quality issues (algal blooms) (World Commission on Dams, 2000b).

Positive externalities

- The dam is a major tourist destination in South Africa – up to 200 000 visitors a year.
- Lake Gariep inland fishery contributes to the livelihoods of the rural poor, who use the lake on a subsistence basis.
- Power generation of the Gariep Dam is 6% higher than the projected power generation since its commissioning in 1998.
- Flow regimes of the Orange River have stabilised.
- There are indirect positive impacts on agriculture, downstream markets, cost of production changes, employment creation, livestock development, etc. (World Commission on Dams, 2000a; World Commission on Dams, 2000b).

Negative externalities

- River regulation has affected three main habitats: dryland habitats, riverine ecosystem and the estuary.
- The dam has displaced 1 260 workers and their families, with female-headed households suffering more than male-headed households (gender issue).
- Blackfly insects have proliferated, which threaten sheep (World Commission on Dams, 2000a; World Commission on Dams, 2000b).

Specific regulations

The release of water from the Gariep Dam is based on hydropower generation (the priority of water use) by the downstream Vanderkloof Dam. The release is scheduled to maximise hydropower generation at the Vanderkloof Dam. (Anon, 2016b) After the release of water to the downstream dam, any surplus water in the reservoir will be released to produce hydropower in the Gariep hydroelectric station. Storage control curves, based on monthly water levels, help determine water levels. Thus, ESKOM can produce power only when the water level is higher than the surplus limit. Operations aim to minimise spill-over and maximise use of the flow.

Future

No information or data available.

6.2. Jebel Aulia, White Nile River Basin, Sudan

Owners, including asset ownership

- Government of Sudan
- National Electricity Corporation (NEC) has authority on hydropower generation.

Physical characteristics

- Volume: 3 500 MCM
- Surface area: 933.4 km^2
- Residence time: 5.9%
- Total internal renewable water resources per capita: 99 m^3/inhabitant/year
- Climatic condition: Arid
- Transboundary users: Egypt (downstream transboundary user).

Key water uses

Irrigation, hydropower, flood and drought risk management.

Irrigation

From 1937 to 1965, until construction of the High Aswan Dam downstream, the reservoir was a storage tank for irrigation. It primarily helped the natural recession for downstream irrigation (Awulachew, 2012; Shahin, 2006).

Hydropower

The dam is equipped with 80 HYDROMATRIX® Turbine Generator (TG) units, which have a total plant capacity of 30.4 MW since 2005 (ANDRITZ Hydro, 2013).

Flood and drought risk management

The dam is used for flood release from time to time. Originally, it was meant to hold back part of the White Nile while the Blue Nile was flooding, and to control White Nile flooding (ANDRITZ Hydro, 2013).

Others

Fisheries in Jebel Aulia accounts for a fish landing of 13 000 tons/year (Dumont, 2009).

Goods and services provided

- Hydroelectricity, irrigation, fisheries, flood control.

Stakeholders

Government

- Government of Sudan
- National Electricity Corporation (NEC) of Sudan
- Sudan People's Armed Forces.

Primary users

- Households
- Fishers.

Others

- ANDRITZ Hydro.

Brief history

The Jebel Aulia Reservoir was considered an important storage reservoir on the White Nile during the 1930s. Egypt approved the project in 1914, but construction was delayed due to World War I. In 1919, the Sudan Construction Company resumed construction, although it halted from time to time due to post-war disputes. (Wikipedia, 2016b) Gibson and Pauling Company (Foreign) Ltd. built the Jebel Aulia Dam between 1933 and 1937. (Mills, 2015); (Wikipedia, 2016c) Initially, the dam acted as an irrigation storage tank and a flood control facility. However, after construction of the Aswan High Dam in 1964, its role diminished. (EzEldin, 2008) In 2005, a hydroelectric project with a capacity of 30 MW was added at the dam.

Business model for MPWI financing, including cost recovery

The Egyptian government financed the project. The Egyptian parliament approved EGP 4.5 million for construction. However, the actual cost was EGP 200 000 less than estimated.

In the context of cost recovery, Jebel Aulia was not able to immediately lead to extension of Egyptian irrigation lands. Jebel Aulia had become a financially burdensome project to Egypt due to the little benefit gained by the country.

Sudan's electricity tariff ranges USD 0.034 kWh/month to USD 0.059 kWh/month.

Key challenges

- Rapid siltation of the reservoir.
- Construction of the Aswan High Dam, which eliminated the irrigation function of the Jebel Aulia Dam.
- The Grand Ethiopian Renaissance Dam, under construction in Ethiopia upstream of the Jebel Aulia Dam, could activate seismic activity in the region due to 63 billion tons of weighing silt and water.

Positive externalities

- Use of the dam to plant HYDROMATRIX® power generating turbines: this is a classic example of adapting an existing irrigation dam structure for hydropower generation. It is a source of low-cost, environmentally-friendly and time-efficient hydropower generation (ANDRITZ Hydro, 2013).
- Source of inland fisheries.

Negative externalities

- The estimated evaporative loss ranging from 2.1 km^3/year to 3.45 km^3/year due to the flat and open nature of the valley above the dam.
- Inadequate storage capacity for land irrigation.
- Displacement of tribes along the White Nile due to filling of the reservoir (Barbour, 1959).

Specific regulations

The hydropower generation turbines at the dam are equipped with HYDROMATRIX®, a new concept of hydraulic energy generation. Turbine units are fitted as one power module containing two turbines and fixed to the upstream face of the dam as gated structures. If the flood release from the reservoirs is higher than the capacity of the modules, gantry cranes will lift the modules.

Future

In February 2016, the President of Sudan stated the importance of expanding the Jebel Aulia Dam in southern Khartoum State (allAfrica.com, 2016).

6.3. Lake Lagdo, Beneu River Basin, Cameroon

Owners, including asset ownership

- Cameroon government
- International power company AES SONEL runs the hydroelectric station.

Physical characteristics

- Volume: 7 800 MCM
- Surface area: 622.6 km^2
- Residence time: 109.2%
- Total internal renewable water resources per capita: 11 695 m^3/inhabitant/year
- Climatic condition: Tropical wet and dry
- Transboundary users: Nigeria.

Key water uses

Irrigation, hydropower.

Irrigation

Area under irrigation using the lake is 1 000 ha, while the total irrigable area is 40 000 ha (Toro, 1997).

Hydropower

Lake Lagdo has an installed capacity of 72 MW to generate electricity by its four turbines, releasing water at a rate of 230 m^3/s (Toro, 1997).

Others

Lake Lagdo accounts for an inland reservoir fishery where the annual yield averages around 200 kg/ha.

Goods and services provided

Hydroelectricity, irrigation, fisheries.

Stakeholders

Government

- Cameroon government
- Government agencies.

Primary users

- Households
- Cameroon farmers

- Downstream communities
- Fishing communities.

Others

- Upstream communities
- Tourists
- Non-government agencies
- Research agencies
- AES SONEL.

Brief history

Lake Lagdo was built on Benue River in Cameroon between 1977 and 1982 to provide electricity to northern Cameroon. Lake Lagdo was financed from Chinese development assistance to Cameroon. The China International Water and Electric Corporation managed construction whose fleets included both Chinese and Cameroonian workers (Wikipedia, 2016d).

Business model for MPWI financing, including cost recovery

The Lake Lagdo project was financed by the Chinese government with a USD 75 million loan provided in 1977. Average electricity tariff is USD 0.19/kWh, while the generation cost is USD 0.25/kWh.

Key challenges

- Significant alteration of the River Benue floodplain downstream of the dam.
- Increased human pressure on natural resources in the floodplain due to immigration of displaced people from the flooded areas of Lake Lagdo.
- Erosion of steep riverbanks when water is released from Lake Lagdo.
- Tendency of flood disasters for Nigeria (downstream country) due to release of water from Lake Lagdo during peak rainfall periods. In 2012, water released from the dam caused floods that led to 10 deaths, submergence of 10 000 homes and 10 000 ha of damaged farmlands. Nigeria has proposed to build the Dasin Hausa Dam to control floods that occur due to water released from Lake Lagdo.
- The ability of Lake Lagdo to be a source of conflict if it is not operated equitably and fairly (i.e. reducing total volume of water flowing into Nigeria).
- Failure of Cameroonian authorities to adopt an operating schedule acceptable by Nigeria as the downstream neighbour.
- Siltation of the downstream riverbed due to less river flow.
- Exclusion of local people from planning and design of actions (e.g. irrigation development) after construction of the reservoir.
- Threat to the water-supply intake points along the river and related irrigation pumping stations due to a drop in the river flow rate (Toro, 1997; Roggeri, 2013).

Positive externalities

- Diminishing of flood peaks after the reservoir impoundments and transformation of the floodplain to a large-scale irrigation development scheme, which extends to thousands of hectares.
- Increase in river flow during the dry seasons (prior to construction of the lake, dry-season flows in November-June were 10-20 m^3/s). Since releases from the dam began in 1984, average low flows recorded are about 60 m^3/s, an increase of over 300%.
- Shift of crops from sorghum to rice.
- Significant fisheries and aquaculture activities in the reservoir.

Negative externalities

- The lake has significantly altered the hydrology and ecology of the downstream floodplain. Changes in the floodplain have affected flood-recession cultivation of sorghum (yearly floods and clayey soils have made the land highly suitable for sorghum cultivation).
- Also, alteration of the floodplain has resulted in less fish production.
- Malaria and schistosomiasis have spread among resettled communities in the floodplain (East bank of the Benue River) due to poor management of water supply and drainage.
- Flooding in Nigeria due to water released from Lake Lagdo. In 2007, opening of Lake Lagdo release gates resulted in a flash flood in Adamawa State, Nigeria, and killed 23 people, while flooding three local government areas (Olaore and Aja 2014).
- Downstream siltation.
- Navigation constraints in the downstream due to decreased water level.

Specific regulations

Several approaches have been taken to mitigate the effects of large-scale interventions of Lake Lagdo and to develop livelihoods of resettled communities. These focus on developing sustainable ways to use the new environment such as in "Project Pisciculture Lagdo (1987-1992)" in Gounougou.

According to an agreement signed in 2007 between the Nigerian and Cameroon governments, Nigeria purchases electricity generated from the Lagdo Dam (International Rivers Africa Program, 2010).

Future

- The World Bank is funding a second phase of the "Niger Basin Water Resources Development and Sustainable Ecosystems Management" project. This will likely lead to rehabilitation and possibly increasing the height of Lagdo Dam in northern Cameroon. This aims to increase the dam's hydropower and irrigation capacity.
- The Cameroon government is looking forward to the potential of promoting and developing tourism based on Lagdo Lake and Dam (Frida-Tolonen, 2014).

6.4. Lake Manantali, Senegal River Basin, Mali

Owners, including asset ownership

The dam is managed by the tripartite Manantali Energy Management Company (the *Société de gestion de l'énergie de Manantali* – SOGEM), which was created in 1997. A 1978 convention on legal status and a 1982 convention on financing established that member states jointly own the Manantali Dam through their shares in SOGEM. (Gakusi, Delponte and Houetohossou, 2015) SOGEM has a 15-year contract with the private company *Eskom Energie Manantali* (EEM), a subsidiary of the South African national power company ESKOM, to operate the plant and manage infrastructure (Wikipedia, 2016e).

Physical characteristics

- Volume: 11 270 MCM
- Surface area: 438.4 km^2
- Residence time: 141.7%
- Total internal renewable water resources per capita: 3 409 m^3/inhabitant/year
- Climatic condition: Semi-arid
- Transboundary users: Mauritania and Senegal.

Key water uses

Irrigation, hydropower.

Irrigation

The dam irrigates 78 100 ha of land in Senegal (54 700 ha), Mauritania (20 400 ha) and Mali (3 000 ha) (Wikipedia, 2016e).

Hydropower

The dam generates 740 GWh of hydroelectricity annually. The production is distributed to Mali (55%), Senegal (30%) and Mauritania (15%) (Wikipedia, 2016e).

Others

Drinking water supply to Dakar, the capital of Senegal.

Goods and services provided

Irrigation, electricity; regulation of the Senegal River to St. Louis and Ambidédi throughout the year; supply of freshwater for the Lac de Guiers, which is a source of the freshwater supply for Dakar, the capital of Senegal; annual recharge of *Lac R'Kiz* and *Aftout es Sahel* in Mauritania to create an artificial estuary.

Stakeholders

Government

- Mali government
- Mauritanian government
- Senegal government
- Government agencies
- *Société de gestion de l'énergie de Manantali* (SOGEM)
- *Organisation pour la mise en valeur du fleuve Sénégal* (OMVS).

Primary users

- Mali farmers
- Mauritanian farmers
- Senegal farmers
- Downstream communities
- Households (potable water users)
- Fishing communities.

Others

- Upstream communities
- Tourists
- Non-government agencies
- Research agencies.

Brief history

Mali, Mauritania and Senegal set up the Organization for the Development of the Senegal River (*Organisation pour la mise en valeur du fleuve Sénégal*, or OMVS) for developing hydropower and irrigation in the basin. As part of the OMVS agenda, the dam was planned over Senegal River in 1972, but construction could not begin due to lack of funds. In 1979, the World Bank declined funding for dam construction, highlighting the unreasonable investment. After securing financial aid from Europe, construction of the dam began in 1982 (Wikipedia, 2016e).

The dam was completed in 1988. At the same time, another dam was built downstream in the Lower Senegal River's delta to prevent backwater flows. Due to lack of funds, the Manantali Dam was built without the hydropower plant. It got further delayed due to the Mauritania-Senegal border war in 1989 and disagreement on transmission line setup. In 1997, OMVS acquired a new loan package to include hydropower generation facilities to the dam, which resulted in Manantali Dam producing hydropower in 2001.

Business model for MPWI financing, including cost recovery

The total cost of the dam (including the hydropower plant) was EUR 1.02 billion. It was financed by 16 donors, including German and French development co-operation, the African Development Bank, World Bank, the European Investment Bank, Canada, Saudi Arabia, Kuwait and the United Nations Development Programme. Mali, Mauritania and Senegal also made financial contributions as beneficiary countries of the project. Soft loans represented 64% of the foreign financing, while the remainder was from grants.

The cost of the hydroelectric station was roughly EUR 320 million. This was funded by 10 donors that included French Development Agency (AFD), World Bank, Kredistanstadt fur Wiederaufbau (KfW, Germany), Canadian International Development Agency, European Union, European Investment Bank, Islamic Development Bank, African Development Bank, Arab Fund for Economic and Social Development and the West African Development Bank.

A cost-benefit sharing methodology developed by Utah State University categorised benefits as irrigation, energy production and navigation. These benefits were then divided among member states using a fixed quota (called "the key"), which could be adjusted.

OMVS Interconnected Network Tariff Protocol was developed to allocate electricity to national electricity companies that manage consumption and payment of electricity tariffs. EEM collects payment from national electricity companies and provides revenues to SOGEM after deducting a contract fee. Overall, the financial and economic indicators of the MPWI are encouraging. The economic rate of return for the project is 15.9% and the financial rate of return is 7% per annum (Gakusi, Delponte and Houetohossou, 2015).

Key challenges

- The dam failed to solve electric power supply issues in the three countries. This has led to power outages and continuous diminishing of the national grid's voltage. As a result, many industries in these countries rely upon their own production of power.
- Plans to develop navigation as a service from the reservoir were abandoned due to their non-feasibility.
- Construction of the dam has affected downstream agricultural activities, which were based on floodplain recession agriculture. The project is estimated to reduce flooding in 30 000 ha of floodplains and reduce pastureland for livestock. There is a 15-year plan to create artificial floods downstream of the dam (Degeorges and Reilly, 2006).
- Regulation and minimisation of potential conflicts can occur between transboundary users.
- Although performance so far has been good, there are risks to sustainability. These touch various issues: technical (lack of an adequate distribution network for electricity), financial (debt payments) and institutional (political instability in some project member countries).

Positive externalities

- Hydropower generation of the dam has exceeded the 540 GWh power production expectation.
- Lake Manantali produces 65-86 kg/ha/year of fish.

Negative externalities

- The construction and filling of the reservoir led to displacement of 10 000 people.
- Most of the 12 000 people forced to resettle have not received sufficient land and agricultural support. Peasant families who had lived in the Senegal Valley for many decades could not afford the shift to irrigated farming.
- The agricultural command area of the dam has been below expectations. Only about 100 000 ha of the planned 375 000 ha has been irrigated so far. Approximately 2 000 ha is added each year.
- Violent conflicts occurred at the regional level due to land legislation reforms that contradicted traditional land rights (e.g. killing of Senegalese farmers by Mauritanians, 1989).
- Impact on flood-recession agriculture, fishing and cattle grazing: fewer floods led to less production of the staple food (sorghum) in the floodplains.
- Diminishing flood cycles have depleted groundwater, leading to destruction and damage of forest cover of nearly 120 km^2.
- Destruction of extensive fish habitats in the floodplains from reduced annual flood events ultimately reduced the riverine fish production.
- Loss of floodplains had long-term adverse impacts on migratory birds (International Rivers Africa Program, 2016).
- Waterborne diseases infested the Senegal River Valley (schistosomiasis and malaria).

Specific regulations

The OMVS, made up of Mali, Mauritania and Senegal, has full legal capacity and power to manage the Senegal River Basin. The basin is governed by two major agreements, both signed in Nouakchott, Mauritania on 11 March 1972: the Convention Concerning the Status of the Senegal River (*Convention Relative au Statut du Fleuve Sénégal*) ("Senegal River Convention"), and the Convention Establishing the Organization for the Development of the Senegal River (*Convention Portant Création de l'Organisation pour la Mise en Valeur du Fleuve Sénégal*) ("OMVS Convention"). Among other smaller agreements is the Convention Establishing the Agency for the Management of Power of Manantali, signed on 7 January 1997 (*Convention Portant Création de l'Agence de Gestion de l'Energie de Manantali*).

At the same time, the OMVS council acts as the "General Assembly" SOGEM to oversee the Manantali Dam project (SOGEM, 2016; Fraval et al., 2002).

Future

OMVS is looking forward to environmental feasibility studies of the Manantali II programme. With implementation of the second phase, SOGEM will upgrade existing facilities and expand transmission to deliver power to adjacent energy-deficient countries.

6.5. Lake Assad (Tabqa Dam), Euphrates River Basin, Syria

Owners, including asset ownership

Syrian government.

Physical characteristics

- Volume: 11 600 MCM
- Surface area: 636.8 km^2
- Residence time: 51.3%
- Total internal renewable water resources per capita: 386 m^3/inhabitant/year
- Climatic condition: Arid
- Transboundary users: Turkey (upstream), Iraq (downstream)
- Lake Assad is the largest water reservoir in Syria (Wikipedia, 2016f).

Key water uses

Irrigation, hydropower.

Irrigation

124 000 ha of land is irrigated with water from Lake Assad (Wikipedia, 2016g).

Hydropower

The hydroelectric station of the dam contains eight Kaplan turbines, each with a potential of 103 MW.

Others

Lake Assad provides 80 MCM of drinking water to Aleppo annually, through a pipeline. The reservoir facilitates an industrial-scale inland fishery.

Goods and services provided

Irrigation, electricity, drinking water, fisheries.

Stakeholders

Government

- Syrian government
- Turkish government
- Iraqi government.

Primary users

- Farmers
- Users of electricity

- Households
- Fishers.

Others

- Militant groups
- Researchers.

Brief history

Discussions for building a dam over Euphrates started as early as 1927 when Syria was a French mandate. After independence in 1946, Syria again looked at the feasibility of the dam. According to an agreement reached between the Syrian government and the Soviet Union in 1957, the latter provided technical and financial aid to build a dam on the Euphrates. In 1960, as a member of the United Arab Republic (UAR), Syria signed an agreement with West Germany for a loan to finance construction of the dam. This arrangement was terminated by the departure of Syria from UAR in 1961. In 1965, Syria came to a new agreement with the Soviet Union on financing the dam, while creating a government department to oversee its construction. The dam, designed mostly for irrigation on both sides of Euphrates and hydropower production, was built from 1968 to 1973; the power station was completed in 1977.

In 2013, a Syrian militant group captured the dam, but the dam's original staff continued to maintain operations.

Business model for MPWI financing, including cost recovery

Total cost of the dam was USD 340 million; USD 100 million took the form of a loan from the Soviet Union. The Soviet Union also provided technical expertise.

Key challenges

- The south-eastern Anatolia Project (GAP) is a multi-purpose water resources development project in the Turkish part of the Euphrates-Tigris River Basin. It could increase the risk of not meeting the potential energy production by the Tabqa hydroelectric station due to the upstream river flow regulations (Tilmant, 2007).
- Diminishing water flow from Turkey (upstream) could make it difficult to reach the full economic potential of the dam. Due to lower than expected water flow from Turkey, as well as lack of maintenance, the hydroelectric station only generates 150 MW instead of 800 MW.
- A dispute arose between Iraq and Syria because the filling of Lake Assad reduced the flow of Euphrates to Iraq. This almost led to a war between the two countries.
- The lake has become a hostage to militant groups of the Syrian Civil War (Mail Online, 2016).
- The projected target of 640 000 ha of irrigated land will not be met.
- The irrigation scheme of Lake Assad suffers from high gypsum content in the reclaimed soils around Lake Assad, soil salinisation and collapse of canals that distribute the water from Lake Assad.

- There is no legal framework for integrated water resources management in Syria (Wikipedia, 2016h).

Positive externalities

- It is one of the major inland fishing grounds of Syria.
- The international effort to excavate and document archaeological remains preserved a significant number of historical artefacts around the future Lake Assad before filling of the reservoir.
- It is an important wintering location for migratory birds.

Negative externalities

- The Keban Dam in Turkey and the Tabqa Dam in Syria caused reduced flows, which increased salinity in the Euphrates water in Iraq (Rahi and Halihan, 2010),.
- An armed conflict between Iraq and Syria nearly resulted in 1975 after impoundment of Lake Assad diminished water flow to Iraq (Kaya, 1998).
- The high average summer temperature of Syria causes high annual evaporation (1.3 km^3/year) from the reservoir.

Specific regulations

According to an agreement between the Syrian Arab Republic and Iraq (1990), Syria agrees to share the Euphrates water with Iraq on a 58% (Iraq) and 42% (Syria) basis. Turkey has only agreed to guarantee 50% of the natural flow of Euphrates River at the Syrian border (Wikipedia, 2016i).

Future

Information is not available.

6.6. Gandhi Sagar, Chambal River Basin, Madhya Pradesh, India

Owners, including asset ownership

Operated and maintained by the Water Resources Department, Government of Madhya Pradesh, India (Central Water Commission, 2012).

Physical characteristics

- Volume: 7 322.8 MCM (Wikipedia, 2016j)
- Surface area: 523.5 km^2/723 km^2
- Residence time: 79.6%
- Total internal renewable water resources per capita: 1 103 (m^3/inhabitant/year)
- Climatic condition: Semi-arid (Wikipedia, 2016k)
- Transboundary users: *not applicable.*

Key water uses

Irrigation, hydropower.

Irrigation

The water released after power generation is used to irrigate 427 000 ha (1.06 million acres) by the Kota Barrage. It is located 104 km downstream of the dam, near the city of Kota in the state of Rajasthan.

Hydropower

The dam supports a 115 MW hydroelectric station with five generating units of 23 MW each, providing a total energy generation of about 564 GWh per annum.

Others

The dam's reservoir area attracts many migratory and non-migratory birds throughout the year. The International Bird Life Agency has qualified the reservoir under "A4iii" criteria, as the congregation of water birds is reported to exceed 20 000 at some points.

Goods and services provided

Irrigation, hydropower, fishing grounds, winter grounds for migratory birds.

Stakeholders

Government

- Water Resources Department
- Irrigation Administration
- Command Area Development Agency.

Primary users

- Farmers
- Users of hydroelectricity
- Fishers
- Fishing co-operatives.

Others

- Citizen forums
- Academics
- Media
- Tourists.

Brief history

Indian Prime Minister Pandit Jawaharlal Nehru initiated the dam in 1954. The Gandhi Sagar Dam, constructed in phase I of a three-phase development plan, was completed in 1960. The three developmental stages were commissioned in 1951 for the Chambal River Valley Development, under the First Five Year Plan launched by the Indian government. In phase I, along with the Gandhi Sagar Dam, the Kota Barrage was built 104 km downstream to provide irrigation water to Rajasthan. In phase II, the Rana Pratap Singh Dam was built 48 km downstream using water released from Gandhi Sagar Dam. In phase III, another dam between Gandhi Sagar Dam and Kota Barrage was built (Mandsaur, 2016).

Business model for MPWI financing, including cost recovery

Total expenditure on construction of the Gandhi Sagar Dam and Power Station was about INR 184 million, out of which construction of the power station cost INR 48 million.

Irrigation water prices in Madhya Pradesh range from INR 99/ha to INR 741/ha. Paddy (INR 198/ha), wheat (INR 24/ha) and sugarcane (INR 741/ha) have crop-specific rates for irrigation water prices (Albiac-Murillo, 2015).

Electricity tariff in India ranges from USD 5.5 cents/kWh to USD 11.3 cents/kWh (Faisal, 2012).

Key challenges

- Gandhi Sagar Reservoir attained its full storage capacity after only five years of its first five decades of operation. The reservoir can fill up only partly because of meagre inflows from upstream, which are due, in turn, to large changes in the upstream catchment. (Gupta and Kawadia, 2003) Estimated water runoff during planning of the reservoir was 3 454-3 947 m^3, while the actual runoff has been 3 207 m^3. This runoff is not sufficient to meet the 7 746 m^3 capacity of the reservoir.
- The energy generation of all three power plants in the Chambal River Valley has declined by 25% relative to the projected 50-year figures.
- According to a hydrographic survey in 2001, the average rate of sedimentation during the first 41 years is 5.508 ha-m/100 km^2/year. This is far different from initial predictions of 3.6308 ha-m/100 km^2/year (Jain, Agarwal and Singh, 2007).

Positive externalities

- The Gandhi Sagar wildlife sanctuary at the Gandhi Sagar Reservoir (notified in 1974) offers abundant opportunities of sighting a variety of wildlife (Wikipedia, 2016l).
- The reservoir area attracts many migratory and non-migratory birds throughout the year.
- The International Bird Life Agency has qualified the reservoir under "A4iii" criteria, as the congregation of water birds is reported to exceed 20 000 at some points.
- Commercial fisheries were initiated in 1959-60 in Gandhi Sagar, and have been credited as the best-managed reservoir in the state.
- The fisheries production of Gandhi Sagar is 607 tonnes annually with a fish yield of 9.21 kg/ha (Petr, 2003).

Negative externalities

- To maintain inflows into the reservoir, surface water harvesting in the catchment area of Gandhi Sagar has been banned. This has led to unequal distribution of the net gains between Madhya Pradesh and Rajasthan states from the Chambal Valley Development Project.
- The banning of surface water abstraction has resulted in an unbalanced development of irrigation facilities in the catchment districts.
- Due to the ban on surface water abstraction in Madhya Pradesh, groundwater irrigation has increased. This has led to a falling groundwater table in some districts (by up to 15 metres in 15 years) (Gupta, Kawadia and Attari, 2007).

Specific regulations

To maintain the maximum water runoff to the Gandhi Sagar Reservoir, the government of Madhya Pradesh has banned harvesting any surface water in the catchment area of the Gandhi Sagar. This area is spread over 22 500 km^2 in eight districts of Malwa, namely Dhar, Indore, Dewas, Shajapur, Ujjain, Ratlam, Mandsaur and Neemuch.

Future

Some organisations suggest the full reservoir level in the Gandhi Sagar Dam can be reduced without affecting operations. Studies show that reducing the full reservoir level from 1 312 feet to 1 295 feet (400 m to 394 m) could enable about 40 000 ha of presently submerged land for cultivation by farmers who originally owned these lands (Himanshu, 2010).

6.7. Hirakud Lake, Mahanadi River Basin, India

Owners, including asset ownership

Government of Odisha State.

Physical characteristics

- Volume: 8 141 MCM (original)/5 896 MCM (revised in 2000)
- Surface area: 500.7 km^2/743 km^2
- Residence time: 23.1%
- Total internal renewable water resources per capita: 1 103 (m^3/inhabitant/year)
- Climatic condition: Tropical wet
- Transboundary users: N/A
- The dam is the longest earthen dam, and the reservoir one of the largest artificial lakes, in Asia (Choudhury, Sandbhor and Satapathy, 2012).

Key water uses

Irrigation, hydropower, flood and drought risk management.

Irrigation

The project provides 1 556 km² of *Kharif* (monsoon) and 1 084 km² of *Rabi* (spring) irrigation in the districts of Sambalpur, Bargarh, Bolangir and Subarnpur in the state of Orrisa.

Hydropower

The dam has a capacity to generate up to 307.5 MW of electrical power through its two power plants.

Hydroelectric station (HES) I is located at the base (toe) of the main dam section and contains 3 x 37.5 MW Kaplan turbine and 2 x 24 MW Francis turbine generators with a total installed capacity of 259.5 MW. HES II is located 19 km (12 miles) southeast of the dam at Chipilima. It contains 3 x 24 MW generators.

Flood and drought risk management

The construction of the dam has alleviated periodic droughts in the upper drainage basin of Mahanadi River, as well as flooding in the lower delta regions that were subjected to crop damage.

The dam controls flooding of the Mahanadi delta by regulating 83 400 km² of Mahanadi drainage (Wikipedia, 2016m).

It provides flood protection to 9 500 km² of delta area in districts of Cuttack and Puri.

Others

Navigation.

Goods and services provided

Irrigation water supply, electricity, flood protection, drinking water, water and electricity for the downstream industries (paper mills, aluminum, rice mills, cement production, sugar mills).

Stakeholders

Government

- State agencies dealing with water, foremost the Water Resources Department, Irrigation Administration, Command Area Development Agency, *Pani Panchayats* (Water Users' Associations, or WUAs) to manage irrigation water, and Soil Conservation Department
- Agricultural Department, including Agricultural Technology Management Agency (ATMA), soil testing laboratory, Sambalpur and Organic Farming Unit
- *Panchayati Raj* institutions and representatives (for village-level governance and conflict resolution).

Primary users

- Farmers
- Industries
- Fishers.

Others

- Associations, such as farmers' unions, WUAs and other civil society organisations
- Academics and environmentalists (individuals)
- Media (print and audio-visual media).

Brief history

Since 1868, there have been as many as 39 floods in the Mahanadi Delta, as well as significant periodic droughts in the upstream of Mahanadi. Such floods and droughts necessarily caused insecurity to human life and property. They had a demoralising effect on inhabitants and shattered their enthusiasm to improve the land. (Baboo, 1991) The dam was constructed to address the issues of floods in the Mahanadi Delta and to benefit from controlling the Mahanadi River for multi-purpose use. The work took place from 15 March 1946 to 13 January 1957. Power generation along with agricultural irrigation started in 1956, achieving full potential in 1966. The Hirakud Dam and Reservoir have been viewed as a symbol of India's post-independence *developmentalism.*

Business model for MPWI financing, including cost recovery

The total capital cost of the project is LKR 1 000.2 million (in 1957). Cost recovery was not specified at the commissioning of the reservoir. The project focused on benefiting downstream communities, while protecting Mahanadi coastal communities from flooding. However, several policies have been implemented to streamline the use of the Hirakud reservoir.

Until 1990, water from the dam was mainly for hydropower generation and irrigation. Industrial water use was minimal during that period. Flood control has been the major purpose of the project since then. A rule curve committee was appointed in 1988 to lower the water level of the reservoir during the monsoon period as near to the dead storage level as possible for flood control.

Key challenges

- Protests: the anti-Hirakud Dam campaign has been ongoing since the decision to build the dam was announced in 1945. The project has fallen far behind schedule during construction. This has resulted in more capital costs, interest charges and delayed returns.
- Compensation strategies are needed for displaced village communities (Baboo, 1991).
- Farmers in the Hirakud command are in conflict with the government of Odisha over allocation of water from the reservoir to industries. Industry and the agricultural community are in conflict about water allocation strategies.

- The electricity generation from the dam is only 62.24% of the original claims.
- The irrigated area is 55.85% of the initial target.
- The limited storage of the reservoir in relation to the size of its catchment has substantial effects on Hirakud's flood control objectives.
- The hydrologic impact of climate change is likely to decrease performance of, and annual hydropower generation by, the Hirakud reservoir. Mean monthly storages are likely to decrease in future scenarios. In many scenarios for 2075-95, the reservoir is unable to get filled by the end of the monsoon in October.
- High silt flows into the Hirakud reservoir due to considerable deforestation in the upper catchment area.
- Over half a century after construction of the dam, its catchment, reservoir and command have undergone considerable economic and ecological changes. These changes have significantly affected water use and availability, both in terms of quality and quantity, as well as inflows into, and outflows from, the dam.
- Illegal fishing has led to overexploitation of the fish resource in the reservoir.
- Polluted water discharged by industries upstream degrades water quality in the reservoir.
- Navigation in the reservoir, which was an initial objective, has still not materialised.

Positive externalities

- The reservoir provides a sufficient supply of water for drinking and sanitation.
- The reservoir is a destination for migratory birds from Caspian Sea, Lake Baikal, Aral Sea, Mongolia, Central and Southeast Asia, and the Himalaya region (Times of India, 2012).
- Water released by the power plant irrigates another 4 360 km² of cultivable land area in the Mahanadi Delta.
- Hirakud reservoir comprises a fishery with an annual average yield of 6.6 kg/ha (151.54 tonnes in 2004/05). The fish catch is made up of 40 commercial fish species with a 239 kg catch per unit effort.

Negative externalities

- Construction of the dam has affected 249 villages and 22 144 families. Significant numbers of individuals were displaced. This resulted in severe livelihood crises, health hazards and diseases in the initial period of their self-resettlement.
- Rates of compensation were much less than the market value of property lost by displaced people.
- Hirakud Dam has arguably submerged more lands and displaced more people than estimated in the feasibility report (Nayak, 2010).
- Most post-Hirakud floods have been attributed to mismanagement of reservoir operations.
- Following commissioning of the reservoir, the number of industries has grown. Concentration of contaminants in the reservoir water, especially mercury, chlorine, fluoride and fly ash, has also increased, affecting fish diversity and catch significantly.

- The dam has reduced inflow, increased uptake by industries from specific locations, increased siltation and changed spatial spread with seasons.
- Poor water allocation strategies and regular canal repairing processes result in shortages of irrigation water from time to time.
- Environmental flow is insufficient.

Specific regulations

The main objective of the Hirakud Dam was flood control; irrigation and hydropower generation were secondary. To make the reservoir more economical, the dam planners designed it as a multi-purpose project that would provide other benefits as well. To that end, it must keep the water level in the reservoir as low as possible in the monsoon period. This will allow floodwater to be stored and discharged in a regulated manner. Also, the dam needs to be filled to its Full Reservoir Level (FRL) by the end of the monsoon to provide water for irrigation, drinking and hydropower generation.

A rule curve committee raises and lowers reservoir levels in specific periods. In this way, they control floods and assure water is available in the reservoir at the end of the monsoon for other purposes.

After 1990, new legislation set priorities for water use for different sectors to supplement the River Board Act (1956). These new acts are: State Water Policy (1994), Orissa Pani Panchayat Act and Rule (2002), State Water Plan (2004), Pani Panchayat Act (2005) and State Water Policy (2007). The last-mentioned act replaces legislation from 1994.

These acts identify management strategies and tariffs for use of the Hirakud Reservoir and its water. The Odisha State Water Policy (2007) set drinking water as the top priority, followed by the environment, irrigation and power; industry is the fifth priority. In 2004, the state developed a new reservoir fishing policy, which increased the leasing tariff and brought in provisions.

Future

- Underwater scans at Hirakud Reservoir have quantified and analysed cracks in the dam to continue with treatment (FAO, India 1994b).
- Discussions are ongoing for a performance evaluation of the Hirakud project, and an assessment of its socio-economic and environmental impacts.
- There are plans to systematically revisit decisions that displaced communities, and consult all relevant stakeholders through a multi-stakeholder consultation, keeping equity and justice at par, if not above, economic and efficiency considerations.

6.8. Iran-Turkmenistan Friendship Dam (Doosti Reservoir)

Owners, including asset ownership

- In Turkmenistan, the owner is the Ministry of Water and Land Reclamation.
- In Iran, the owner is Razavi Khorasan Regional Water Authority.

Physical characteristics

- Volume: 1 250 MCM
- Surface area: 30 km^2
- Residence time: 31.88%
- Total internal renewable water resources per capita: 261 m^3/inhabitant/year (Turkmenistan), 1 624 m^3/inhabitant/year (Iran)
- Climatic condition: Semi-arid
- Transboundary users: Afghanistan (upstream country) in addition to Turkmenistan and Iran.

Key water uses

Irrigation, hydropower.

Irrigation

Out of the 970 MCM inflows to the Doosti Reservoir, 114 MCM are diverted to irrigation schemes in Iran, while 325 MCM are diverted to similar schemes in Turkmenistan.

Hydropower

The dam has a HES with installed capacity of 16 MW provided by three Francis turbines (Wikipedia, 2016n).

Others

Iran receives 178 MCM of water for drinking water supply and industrial purposes; a further 33 MCM are diverted to Iran for artificial recharge.

Goods and services provided

- Irrigation, electricity, drinking water.

Stakeholders

Government

- In Turkmenistan, foremost the Ministry of Water and Land Reclamation
- In Iran, foremost the Razavi Khorasan Regional Water Authority of Iran.

Primary users

- Turkmenistan and Iranian farmers
- Iranian industries
- Turkmenistan and Iranian households.

Others

- Afghan farmers and households
- Research institutes.

Brief history

Since the early 1920s, there have been discussions and disputes between Iran and the Soviet Union regarding the water allocations of Harirud River. In 1921, an agreement between the two defined the allocations. A 1926 agreement on "Exploitation of Border Rivers and Waters along the Harirud to the Caspian Sea" discussed the possibilities of a dam on Harirud River. In 1958, both countries agreed upon a feasibility study for a reservoir, which was conducted from 1974-79. However, the Iranian revolution and the Soviet Union collapse delayed any further action on the dam (Nairizi, 2016).

Later, Turkmenistan and Iran signed a protocol in 1991 for a new feasibility study and to create protocols to construct the dam. Both governments approved the final design in 1999 and a joint management committee was set up the following year. Construction of the dam started in 2001 and was completed in 2005, one year ahead of schedule.

Business model for MPWI financing, including cost recovery

The total cost of the project was USD 168 million. Both Iran and Turkmenistan financed the project equally and are sharing benefits through the joint management committee.

Iran's electricity tariff ranges from USD 2-19 cents/kWh. (Wikipedia, 2016o) Iran's surface water for irrigation is priced between 1% and 3% of the crop value that is cultivated (Keshavarz et al., 2005).

Electricity in Turkmenistan is reportedly distributed free of charge under certain limits, but no information is available on the policy structure. (Inogate, 2015) Water for irrigation is also supplied free in Turkmenistan, which falls into set limits of water supply (EBRD, 2009).

Key challenges

- Transboundary countries lack agreements and legal institutions in Harirud (border) river basin management
- The India-Afghanistan Friendship Dam was built upstream.
- The reservoir uses old cultivation and irrigation systems upstream with low water-use efficiency.
- Language and translation are an issue between the two parties representing the two countries during the management and operational activities of the dam.
- Difficult financial situation and concerns prevail in both countries.
- The reservoir and dam have management and execution issues during operation.
- Evaporation and leakage generate water losses.
- Drought or the seasonality of the river flow: in 2000, the river dried up completely during a ten-month drought.

Positive externalities

- Development: progressive development achieved in the region in the water and energy sectors.
- Political: consolidation of the Iran-Turkmenistan border (Sinaei, 2011).
- The reservoir consolidated and expanded relationships between Iran and Turkmenistan to higher levels.

Negative externalities

- No information available.

Specific regulations

The Common Coordinating Commission (CCC), comprised of representatives from the two countries, initially investigated technical or legal problems that occurred during construction of the dam (see Figure 6.2) (Attarzadeh and Vatanfada, 2011).

The JMC evolved to become the committee responsible for operational activities of the dam. It manages water distribution from the reservoir, environmental flow of Harirud River and a new diversion dam downstream for agriculture use (Vatanfada and Mesgari, 2014).

Figure 6.2. **Doosti Dam Common Coordinating Commission (CCC)**

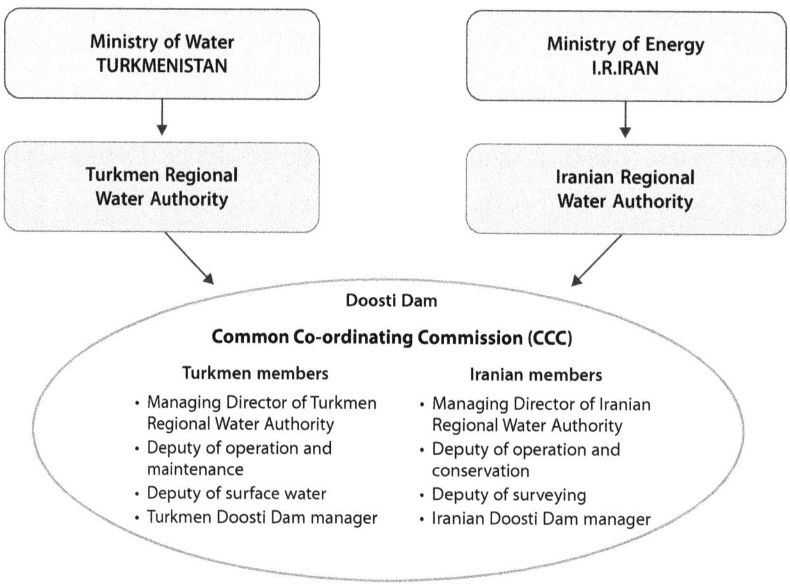

Source: Vatanfada and Mesgari (2014), *Doosti Dam Progress on Water Cooperation.*

Future

Iran, Turkmenistan and Afghanistan are looking forward to trilateral commissions of water and energy as a contribution to regional improvements in water and energy (MEHR, 2016).

6.9. Kapchagay Reservoir, Ili River, Kazakhstan

Owners, including asset ownership

Government of Kazakhstan.

Physical characteristics

- Volume: 28 100 MCM
- Surface area: 1 206 km^2
- Residence time: 2 308.3%
- Total internal renewable water resources per capita: 3 651 m^3/inhabitant/year
- Climatic condition: Semi-arid
- Transboundary users: People's Republic of China (upstream country) in addition to Kazakhstan.

Key water uses

Irrigation, hydropower.

Irrigation

Reservoir provides water for arid irrigation downstream (Wikipedia, 2016p).

Hydropower

Hydropower capacity of the hydroelectric station is 364 MW from four turbines, each with a capacity of 91 MW, generating 972 million KWh of electricity every year (Wikipedia, 2016q).

Others

Other water uses include fishery and leisure.

Goods and services provided

Irrigation, electricity, fisheries, tourism, recreation.

Stakeholders

Government

- Kazakh government
- Chinese government.

Primary users

- Farmers
- Households
- Fishers.

Others

- Almaty Power Consolidated Company
- Tourists
- Non-government agencies
- Research agencies.

Brief history

The former Soviet Union began construction of the Kapchagay Reservoir on Ili River in Kazakhstan in 1967 to develop irrigation in the Lake Balkhash basin. The dam was completed in 1969. The filling of the reservoir, which began in 1970, was expected to take 20 years. The combination of water in the reservoir and drier climatic conditions led to a deep drop in the water table in Lake Balkhash. This had a negative effect on the lake's fragile ecosystem and its surroundings. Due to ecological concerns, the filling of the reservoir was stopped in 1989 and only resumed after the collapse of the Soviet Union. The development of irrigation was also discontinued in the region. This led to reduced human activity and less improvement of the water situation in Lake Balkhash (Aladin and Plotnikov, 1993).

Business model for MPWI financing, including cost recovery

Management of the basin, Kapchagay Reservoir and the Kapchagay HES is not under a single authority and hence not well co-ordinated. The Almaty Power Consolidated Company (APCC) has managed the Kapchagay hydroelectric power station since 1996. In 2007, the company was reorganised and Kapchagay hydroelectric station became part of "Almaty Power Stations". The electricity produced is sold, but farmers do not pay any tariffs for irrigation water from the reservoir.

Key challenges

- The filling of the Kapchagay Reservoir, along with the drastic change in the natural hydrological regime of the Ili River, led to a fall in the water level of Lake Balkhash. This, in turn, resulted in ecological problems and degradation.
- The downfall of the Soviet Union led to economic problems which, in turn, reduced agricultural activities in Kazakhstan.
- Due to its increased economic activity in the Ili-Lake Balkhash Basin, the Chinese government plans to significantly increase its water intake from the Ili River upstream to extend the irrigated area by 450 000 ha. The government also plans to build 15 water reservoirs in the upper flows of all three of Ili's major contributing tributaries. This will further reduce inflow to the Kapchagay Reservoir.
- There are conflicts of interests between different water users (hydropower production and irrigation requirement), with less water released in the summer and more in the winter.
- The administrative system in the post-Soviet Republic of Kazakhstan should be enhanced to provide effective integrated management of water resources.
- Local farmers, being major consumers of the Ili's water, pay no fees for water consumption (i.e. fee for using water as natural resource). Thus, they are not encouraged to introduce efficient technologies for water use (Propastin, 2012).

Positive externalities

- Kapchagay is a tourist attraction in the Almaty region during summer.
- Kapchagay Reservoir is a major fishing ground in the region (Petr, 2003).
- New deltaic regions have been enriched by unique biodiversity.
- New deltas have capacity for vast recreational development.
- The new deltaic region has reclaimed land resources (Starodubtsev and Bogdanets, 2011).

Negative externalities

- The drop in the water level of Lake Balkhash has resulted in the following:
  - Degradation of wetlands in the Lake Balkhash Basin, rising salinity in the lake, decline in fish stocks and an alteration of natural hydrological patterns.

Specific regulations

To reduce ecological degradation of Lake Balkhash due to reduced inflows, the Government of Kazakh Soviet Socialist Republic (KazSSR) stopped filling the Kapchagay Reservoir in 1990. This policy continued until the dissolution of the Soviet Union in 1991 when filling resumed.

In the former Soviet Union, the Ministry of Water Economy (Minvodkhoz) set up distinct water management bodies – *Bassejnovoe Vodnoje Ob'edinenie* (BVO) – in each Central Asian republic. Their mandate was to co-ordinate and supervise the use of waters between republics. They also administered water storage and diversion structures in the concerned river basins.

Future

Development of an improved water management system for the Lake Balkhash Basin.

6.10. Kayrakkum Reservoir, Syr-Darya River Basin, Tajikistan

Owners, including asset ownership

Tajikistan government.

Physical characteristics

- Volume: 3 500 MCM
- Surface area: 933.4 km^2
- Residence time: 5.9%
- Total internal renewable water resources per capita: 7 482 m^3/inhabitant/year
- Climatic condition: Arid
- Transboundary users: Kazakhstan, Kyrgyzstan and Uzbekistan.

Key water uses

Irrigation, hydropower.

Irrigation

Water from Kayrakkum Reservoir irrigates 52 000 ha of rice fields.

Hydropower

The hydroelectric station of the dam owns six Kaplan turbines with a 21 MW capacity each (GIBB & SMEC, 2000).

Others

Annual fish production of the reservoir exceeds an average of 100 tonnes.

Goods and services provided

Irrigation, electricity, fisheries, drinking water, recreation.

Stakeholders

Government

- Tajik government and government agencies.

Primary users

- Farmers
- Fishers
- Downstream communities
- Households.

Others

- Upstream communities
- Tourists
- Non-government agencies
- Research agencies.

Brief history

The construction of the Kayrakkum Dam, designed by SAO GIDROPROEKT Institute in Tashkent, began in July 1951. The construction of the dam involved resettlement of nearly 2 400 families from 20 village areas that were flooded by the reservoir filling. Most resettled families were given lands from the Tajik cotton-producing areas of the northern part of the country. The reservoir started filling in 1956, and was commissioned in 1959. During the Soviet Union era, the reservoir was mainly used for irrigation with power generation as secondary goal, but these priorities reversed after the collapse of the Soviet Union (Wikipedia, 2016r).

Business model for MPWI financing, including cost recovery

As of 2006, Tajikistan was using a uniform tariff rate for irrigation water equivalent to USD 2 per 1 000 m^3 of water, irrespective of source or use of water. This was below the operational cost of the infrastructure. At national level, the government spent roughly USD 1.7 million per year over 2000-04 for improving irrigation and collector-drainage systems. During the same time periods, USD 28.6 per ha of irrigated land was charged as water supply fee, out of which farmers paid 60%.

A two-phase upgrade of the Kayrakkum hydropower plant started in 2015. The total cost of modernisation will be USD 169 million. Phase 1 will cost about USD 50 million, part of which will be funded by the European Bank for Reconstruction and Development. The Pilot Program for Climate Resilience of the Climate Investment Fund will provide a USD 11 million grant and a USD 10 million concessional loan (HydroWorld, 2015).

Key challenges

- Uzbekistan and Tajikistan disagree on both construction of reservoirs in mountainous areas and their operations; Nurek and Kayrakkum reservoirs hold water for irrigation in Uzbekistan, Turkmenistan and Kazakhstan (FAO, 2016).
- The conflict between the need for hydroelectric power generation and irrigation has become a key challenge. Hydropower generation in the winter implies accumulating water (and not releasing enough water) in the summer, when the need for irrigation water is the highest. This has resulted in lost incomes from irrigation in summer due to extensive power generation activities during the winter.
- Bank erosion and submergence of the reservoir shorelines, and changing temperature conditions downstream, have reduced the quality of irrigation water.
- Long-term, continuous siltation has reduced the effective volume and life of the reservoir.
- Water resource planning at national level is not well co-ordinated (Ministry of Irrigation and Water Management of the Republic of Tajikistan, 2006).

Positive externalities

- The additional load and reduced firmness of the Earth crust from moisture reduced seismic activity in adjacent regions.
- The reservoir provides protection against flash floods.
- Improved micro-climates in nearby zones led to improved recreational capacities (CA&CC Press AB, 2016).
- Hatchery facilities have been producing fish fingerlings from reservoir water for many years (Khaitov et al., 2013).
- Commercial-scale fish catches from the reservoir strengthen the reservoir fishery in the area. Also, industries associated with fisheries have been developed.
- BirdLife International has identified a land area of 1 150 km^2, which includes the reservoir and surrounding areas, as an Important Bird Area. It has been designated as a Ramsar site.

Negative externalities

- Continuous siltation of the reservoir could cause water shortages of up to 700 MCM during the irrigation season (Ministry of Irrigation and Water Management of the Republic of Tajikistan, 2006).

Specific regulations

The interstate structures play a key role in managing the waterpower regimes at regional scale. The Syrdarya and Amudarya Basin Hydroeconomic Association manages hydro-economic irrigation facilities. The interstate Hydroeconomic Coordination Commission makes policy, resolves issues and approves annual operational conditions. The Electric Power Council of Central Asia and its executive structure, the Joint Dispatch Control Center (Central Asia JDC), supervise co-ordination of energy systems and sustainability of operations.

Management of the Kayrakkum Reservoir falls under the tripartite agreement between Kazakhstan, Kyrgyzstan and Uzbekistan. Together, they regulate river flow to ensure equity between the three countries for irrigation and hydropower generation (CA&CC Press AB, 2016).

Future

An Austrian consulting firm has signed a contract to modernise the Kayrakkum hydropower facility. Phase 1 will upgrade two of the six units, build capacity of power sector officials and develop a regulatory plan. Phase 2 will create a policy and regulatory body, develop a new tariff methodology and develop legislation for better governance and business conduct of the state-owned power utility company (responsible for operating the hydroelectric station).

6.11. Nurek Reservoir, Vakhsh River, Tajikistan

Owners, including asset ownership

Barqi Tojik (Tajikistan state-owned national integrated power company).

Physical characteristics

- Volume: 10 500 MCM
- Surface area: 62 km^2
- Residence time: 108.8%
- Total internal renewable water resources per capita: 7 482 m^3/inhabitant/year
- Climatic condition: Arid
- Transboundary users: Kyrgyzstan (upstream country), Uzbekistan and Turkmenistan (downstream countries)
- Second tallest dam in the world and the largest reservoir in Tajikistan (Olsson et al., 2008).

Key water uses

Irrigation, hydropower.

Irrigation

The local agricultural lands are irrigated using the reservoir water by transporting water through the Dangara irrigation canal for 14 km and then distributed over an irrigated area of nearly 70 000 ha (700 km^2) (Wikipedia, 2016s).

Hydropower

Nine Francis turbines with a capacity of 300 MW each (2 700 MW total) were installed in the Nurek powerhouse originally. The generation capacity was upgraded to 3 015 MW between 1984-88. With its 4.0 GW hydropower generating capacity, the water infrastructure accounts for 98% of the national electricity produced.

Others

Several aquaculture activities (grow out fishing, cage culture) and fisheries operations are carried out in Nurek Reservoir.

Goods and services provided

Irrrigation, electricity, fishery, recreation.

Stakeholders

Government

- Tajik government
- Barqi Tojik.

Primary users

- Tajik farmers
- Tajik fishers
- Downstream communities
- Households.

Others

- Upstream communities
- Tourists
- Non-government agencies
- Research agencies.

Brief history

Construction of the Nurek Dam on Vashsh River started in 1961. All the power generators were commissioned from 1972 to 1979. The project was completed in 1980. Initially, the dam provided water during irrigation (growth) seasons. At present, the dam releases water for hydropower generation during the winter months.

Business model for MPWI financing, including cost recovery

Barki Tojik sells electricity at a fixed price established by the government. The weighted average tariff in 2006 was USD 0.006/kWh, which was increased to USD 0.015/kWh by 2008. According to Barki Tojik, these tariff levels are unable to cover the operational cost of the power-generating sources (USD 0.030/kWh). In 2010, the government increased the tariff to a weighted average of USD 0.024/kWh.

The Tajik government has also authorised an energy subsidy. This is affecting the pricing structure of electricity, as well as discouraging private sector investors in the electricity sector (ADB, 2015).

Key challenges

- The dissolution of the Soviet Union provoked an economic crisis in Tajikistan. The country depends highly on the Nurek hydropower plant to meet its electricity needs.
- Siltation of the dam is reducing the life of Nurek Reservoir. A World Bank report (2005) states that roughly 50 m of the 300 m has been lost due to silt over the past 25 years.
- There has been continuous seismic activity and moderate earthquakes in the region of the Nurek Reservoir.
- Disputes could erupt between Tajikistan and Uzbekistan, especially if the Rogun Dam, upstream of Nuruk Dam, is constructed. With two MPWIs on the Vakhsh River, Tajikistan will have greater ability to regulate water flow. This will lead to water shortages in Uzbekistan (Votrin, 2003).
- The breakup of the Soviet Union weakened river management institutions. The BVO, a river basin organisation created to control Amu Darya River flow during the Soviet Union, was no exception. It suffered from weak political commitment and co-operation. The organisation was meant to manage water distribution in riparian provinces (Glantz, 2005).

Positive externalities

- Nurek Reservoir has become a major recreation hot spot in Tajikistan for hiking, boating and fishing.
- There is less interdependence between the upstream and downstream control due to the small quantity of Amu Darya Basin water controlled by the Nurek Reservoir.
- Fisheries and aquaculture activities take place in the reservoir (Khaitov et al., 2013).

Negative externalities

- Resettlement of 5 000 people.
- Accumulation of a significant proportion of runoff of the Vakhsh River in the first years of commissioning of the dam (1972).
- More than 1 800 earthquakes occurred within the first nine years of filling Nurek Reservoir. Magnitudes of the quakes ranged between 1.4 and 4.6 degrees on the Richter scale. Seismic activity after filling the reservoir has more than quadrupled (Simpson and Negmatullaev, 1981; Soboleva and Mamadaliev, 1976).

Specific regulations

Nurek Reservoir is regulated to meet its need for supporting downstream irrigated agriculture and production of hydroelectricity. Figure 6.3 indicates daily values of Nurek water levels, inflow and outflow from 2003 to 2004. It shows how the reservoir is managed to use water flow of the Vakhsh River for irrigated agriculture in downstream Turkmenistan and Uzbekistan in a seasonal pattern (Srivastava et al., 1995).

Figure 6.3. **Daily water-level variations, inflow and outflow for Nurek reservoir for 2003 and 2004**

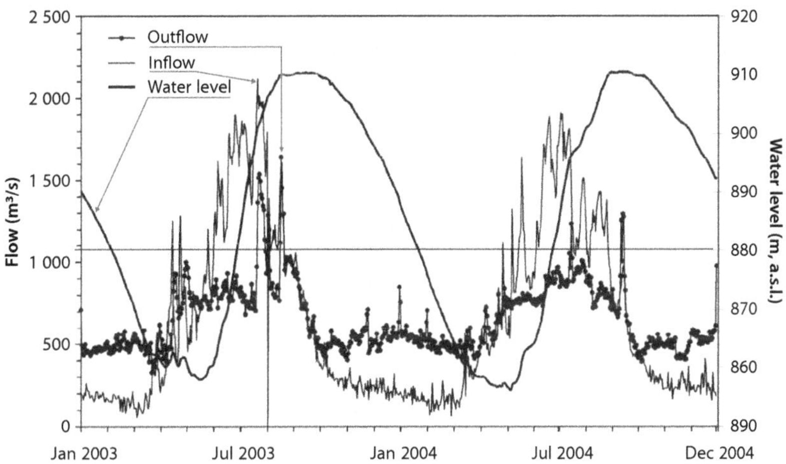

Source: Olsson, O. et al. (2008), *The role of the Amu Darya dams and reservoirs in future water supply in the Amu Darya basin.*

Future

The Rogun Dam, under construction 70 km upstream of Nurek, can trap sediment. Consequently, it is expected to reduce siltation and storage capacity losses of existing downstream reservoirs (Schmidt et al., 2006).

6.12. Toktogul Reservoir, Naryn River, Kyrgyzstan

Owners, including asset ownership

Kyrgyz government.

Physical characteristics

- Volume: 19 500 MCM
- Surface area: 223.5 km^2
- Residence time: 267%
- Total internal renewable water resources per capita: 8 237 m^3/inhabitant/year
- Climatic condition: Arid
- Transboundary users: Kazakhstan and Uzbekistan.

Key water uses

Irrigation, hydropower.

Irrigation

The commissioning of the reservoir has augmented water supply to 800 000 ha of irrigated lands, as well as providing water to 480 000 ha of newly irrigated lands. The irrigated lands are mostly in Uzbekistan and Kazakhstan.

Hydropower

The hydropower capacity of the reservoir is 1 200 MW (four turbines of 300 MW each) while its annual output of electric power is 4 100 million kWh. It provides 90% of the electricity produced in Kyrgyzstan (Kraak, 2012).

Others

The fish catch from Toktogul Reservoir was 150 tons in 2005.

Goods and services provided

Irrigation, electricity, fishery, tourism, recreation.

Stakeholders

Government

- Kyrgyz government and government agencies
- Kazakh government and government agencies
- Uzbek government and government agencies.

Primary users

- Kyrgyz, Kazakh and Uzbek farmers
- Fishers
- Operator of the hydroelectric station
- Industries
- Households.

Others

- Tourists
- Non-government agencies
- Research agencies.

Brief history

The Toktogul Hydraulic System was designed to meet cotton production targets set by the government of the former Soviet Union. It aimed to increase cotton production from 4.3 million tons in 1960 to 8 million tons in 1970, and to 10-11 million tons in 1990. Increased cotton production required extensive construction of irrigation systems, particularly in the Syr Darya River Basin (Uzbekistan and Kazakhstan), the most important region of cotton farming in Central Asia. The Kairakkum water reservoir irrigation depended on the natural flow of the river since there were no regulating reservoirs. Therefore, to implement long-term flow control, Toktogul Reservoir was constructed on the Naryn River. It was designed for an effective storage capacity of 14.0 billion cubic metres (Bm^3) (as determined by irrigation requirements). However, the actual full storage capacity of the reservoir is 19.5 Bm^3 due to water backup into the canyon of the Naryn River, Ketmentiube depression and the valleys of its three tributaries – Uzunakhmat, Chichkan and Torkent.

With the dissolution of the Soviet Union, Kyrgyzstan became an independent country. It suffered from shortages of electricity in the winter; faced the lack of fossil fuels such as oil, coal and natural gas, and high international prices (in hard currency) to import fossil fuels. This led to a serious energy problem, leading Kyrgyzstan to switch the mode of Toktogul Reservoir from irrigation to power generation. The new mode required less release of water in the summer (when downstream irrigation demand is high) and more release of water in the winter (when downstream irrigation demand is low).

Since 1994, Central Asian countries have signed multiple protocols and agreements to develop water and energy in the region. Three agreements, specifically on the use of the Naryn-Syr Darya Cascade of Reservoirs for energy and water, were signed between Kazakhstan, Kyrgyzstan and Uzbekistan in 1998, 1999 and 2000 (CAWATER, 2016a).

Business model for MPWI financing, including cost recovery

Kyrgyzstan sells its generated power, which is distributed to the Kyrgyz population at a low tariff rate. The collection rate, however, is also very low. (Teasley and McKinney, 2011) The hydropower generated by the reservoir has been bartered with the neighbouring countries of Uzbekistan and Kazakhstan in return for natural gas and coal, respectively. (UN Water, 2013) Multiple protocols and agreements have been signed between Kazakhstan,

Kyrgyzstan and Uzbekistan since 1995. They broadly state that excess electricity generated by Kyrgyzstan in summer will be purchased in equal amounts by Kazakhstan and Uzbekistan. These countries, in turn, will provide an equivalent supply of electricity and fuel for the winter needs of Kyrgyzstan.

There is a three-phase Toktogul hydropower plant rehabilitation plan funded by the Asian Development Bank (Toktogul HPP Rehabilitation in Kyrgyz Republic). Phase 1 foresees replacement of the electrical mechanical equipment of the plant). Phase 2 will replace the second and fourth turbine-generator units. The third phase will replace the first and third turbine-generator units (EFSD, 2015).

Key challenges

- The Toktogul Reservoir was commissioned in 1974, but for a long period could not be filled up to the maximum level. Its storage did not exceed 5-6 BM^3. Only after many wet years did the reservoir storage reach 19.5 BM^3 in August 1998.
- With the disintegration of the Soviet Union, the priority of the reservoir switched from water supply primarily for agriculture to hydropower generation. This drastically changed the economic situation in the Syr Darya Basin. Changes in the river regime due to intensive use of water resources for hydroelectric power generation have created serious complications in the basin, both in summer and winter. This has created tension between downstream farmers and upstream hydropower producers. The downstream farmers need more water for irrigation during summer, whereas Toktogul hydroelectric station releases more water in winter, when the demand for electricity is higher.
- The intergovernmental protocols and agreements in sharing the water and energy do not account sufficiently for environmental problems in the watershed. Discharges from the Syr Darya will fall below minimum levels recorded during the past 100 years of observation. Also, these intergovernmental protocols and agreements are still not hard and fast. Most change every year due to incomplete fulfilment of agreements between countries. These agreements only focus on the benefits of energy resources exchange and do not look at the long-term balanced use of water. This can cause early drawdown of the Toktogul Reservoir and huge losses in both the power and water sectors of the republics.

Positive externalities

- Toktogul Reservoir is a tourist destination in Kyrgyzstan.
- Commercial-level fishery activities are carried out in Toktogul Reservoir.

Negative externalities

- Toktogul Reservoir occupies 28 400 ha of land, including 12 000 ha of arable land with 10 700 ha of irrigated areas. Further, 3 767 houses with yards have been moved from the area of flooding. Due to the reservoir, 26 communities were displaced and 8th century AD archaeological sites were lost (Wikipedia, 2016t).
- In the non-growing season of 1999-2000 (from 24 September 1999 to 14 February 2000), the supply of natural gas to the Kyrgyz energy system was terminated. As a result, because of the extra load of the Cascade hydroelectric stations, the

drawdown of water from the Toktogul Reservoir increased in that period by 1.5 Bm^3 against the same period in 1998-99. That caused an additional discharge of water to the Arnasay depression from the Shardara Reservoir (see Chapter 2).

- This pattern of water releases geared towards generating hydroelectric power from the Toktogul Reservoir caused serious problems for downstream riparian states. During the summer, they faced inadequate supplies of water for irrigation. During winter, the irrigation canals and the riverbed were frozen and could not handle the larger volumes of water releases. This caused flooding and the need to divert water to the Arnasay depression further to the west of the river and away from the Aral Sea. The lake formed by such water releases was called Aydarkul. This has aggravated the ecological situation in the lower reaches of Syr Darya Basin (Schmidt-Soltau, 2004).

Specific regulations

During the Soviet era, the Naryn River Cascade of Reservoirs met the water needs of the four republics (Kyrgyzstan, Kazakhstan, Tajikistan, Uzbekistan) in the Syr Darya Basin. In its schedules, it gave priority to irrigated farming. (CAWATER, 2016b) With the dissolution of the Soviet Union, conflicting economic priorities of the independent countries resulted in clashes of interest over discharge schedules of the Toktogul Reservoir. For this reason, since 1993, the Toktogul cascade of reservoirs has sharply increased the volume of water accumulated in reservoirs over the summer and discharged in the winter. This change in scheduling allows Kyrgyzstan to benefit from producing hydroelectricity at winter times when the demand for it is the highest.

By 1990, in the Syr Darya Basin, a water management system had been set up in accordance with the water usage regime. Several big-size reservoirs of long-term and seasonal control regulate water flow in the basin. These reservoirs, Toktogul, Kairakkum, Shardara, Andojan and Charvak, focus on providing irrigation water for Central-Asian republics (Antipova et al., 2002).

To meet Kyrgyzstan's demands for increased supplies of energy resources and the water needs of Kazakhstan and Uzbekistan in the summer, a fuel and energy exchange agreement defined these countries' mutual obligations. Expert work groups representing water authorities and the power industry of the three countries have drawn up a complex plan of water and energy use for the Syr Darya Basin based on the following principles of mutual compensation:

- Electricity generated in the Naryn cascade of hydroelectric stations by Kyrgyzstan beyond its own (national) needs in the summer shall be purchased in equal amounts by Kazakhstan and Uzbekistan.
- Compensation for this quantity shall be made by an equivalent supply of electricity and fuel (coal, gas, etc.) for the winter needs of Kyrgyzstan.
- Protocols and agreements on this basis have been signed annually since 1995. Tajikistan joined the agreement on 17 June 1998.

Future

The Toktogul power plant is being rehabilitated. In 2015, Kyrgyzstan utility Electric Power Plants (EPP) considered bids to replace electrical components, auxiliaries and instrumentation as part of refurbishing the 1 200 MW Toktogul hydroelectric project on Naryn River in Kyrgyzstan (HydroWorld, 2016).

6.13. Lake Tisza (Kisköre Reservoir), Danube Basin, Hungary

Owners, including asset ownership

Hungarian government owns the reservoir.

- Tiszavíz Hydro Power Plants Ltd. owns the Kisköre power plant.

Physical characteristics

- Volume: 228.6 MCM
- Surface area: 119 km^2
- Residence time: 1.4%
- Total internal renewable water resources per capita: 608 m^3/inhabitant/year
- Climatic condition: Humid subtropical
- Transboundary users: Ukraine and Romania (upstream countries), Serbia (downstream country)
- Largest artificial lake and dam in Hungary (Wikipedia, 2016u).

Key water uses

Irrigation, hydropower, flood and drought risk management.

Irrigation

Supports irrigation activities in the Tisza Valley.

Hydropower

The hydropower generation capacity of the dam is 28 MW. It has four turbines each generating 7 MW.

Flood and drought risk management

Reservoir allows flood control by receiving the upstream floods into the reservoir (Chave, 2001).

Others

Reservoir is a major recreation facility in Hungary. There is a ship lock to provide navigational facilities.

Goods and services provided

Irrigation, electricity, food control, recreation, navigation.

Stakeholders

Government

- Ministry of Environment and Water
- National Water Research Centre
- General Inspectorate of Environment Protection and Water
- Ministry of Agriculture and Rural Development.

Primary users

- Farmers
- Households
- Tourists.

Others

- Tiszavíz Hydro Power Plants Ltd.
- Academia.

Brief history

Lake Tisza was built in 1973 as a segment of the Tisza River Flood Control Project. Filling was completed in the 1990s. The initial name of the reservoir was Kisköre Reservoir. The Hungarian government changed it to Lake Tisza as a supportive strategy to improve recreation and tourism based on the reservoir (Wikipedia, 2016v).

Business model for MPWI financing, including cost recovery

As of 1992, the electricity utility company in Hungary has been broken up into two tiers. The upper tier is controlled by the government-owned *Magyar Villamos Müvek Reszvenytarsag* (MVM). It responsible for "financial flow of electricity-based goods and services" (GENI, 2016). MVM buys the electricity produced by individual producers (which form the second tier) and sells it to distribution companies. Tiszavíz Hydro Power Plants Ltd is one of the producers that own the hydropower plant at Tisza. Overall, hydropower production is a very small component of total electricity generation of the country.

Key challenges

- Major cyanide and heavy metal contamination occurred upstream of the reservoir due to a bursting of a cyanide-storing pond in Romania.
- Lake Tisza is threatened by eutrophication (Rátz and Vizi, 2004).
- Turbidity occurs in the lake due to its shallow nature, creating a challenge for tourism development.

Positive externalities

- The reservoir is an economical substitute for Lake Balaton as a recreational hot spot. The government designated it as an official tourism destination in Hungary.
- Environmental education and tourism: Europe's largest freshwater aquarium "Lake Tisza Ecocentre" is situated on a bank of the lake and is fed by lake water of 535 000 litres (Tisza-tavi Okocentrum, 2016).
- The reservoir has helped increase biodiversity. The eastern part of the lake comprises Lake Tisza Bird Reserve where more than 200 species of birds can be observed (FuniQ, 2016).

Negative externalities

- Tendency to eutrophication and turbidity.

Specific regulations

Lake Tisza falls into the transboundary river basin management regimes prevailing in the Tisza River Basin. These regimes address the following significant environmental risks and social concerns related to the basin:

- Excess and shortage of water
- Landslides
- Diffusion of hazardous pollutants
- Economic development potential
- Sustainable agriculture potential.

During the upstream cyanide contamination, as a protective arrangement, the reservoir was locked. The water level of Kisköre Reservoir was raised before the pollution from the Tisza River reached it. The gates of the dam were opened when the pollutants reached the lake, preventing them from contaminating the reservoir (Szabó et al., 2005).

Future

An investment project named Kiskörei Barrage Reconstruction (*Kiskörei Vízlépcső Rekonstrukciója*) was launched in 2014. It will be completed in 2020. Total costs amount to EUR 8.2 billion.

The project focuses on developing several factors of the Kiskore Dam, which include the following:

- Barrage, boatlocks and dam renovation
- Reconstruction of power supply systems
- Renovation of gantry cranes
- Modernisation of hydroelectric station instruments
- Dredging of reservoir (Lovas, 2013).

6.14. Lake Argyle, Ord River Basin, Australia

Owners, including asset ownership

Government of Western Australia owns the assets.

Pacific Hydro Pty Ltd. manages and controls the hydroelectric station.

Physical characteristics

- Volume: 10 800 MCM
- Surface area: 829.2 km^2
- Residence time: 143.7%
- Total internal renewable water resources per capita: 20 527 m^3/inhabitant/year
- Climatic condition: Tropical wet and dry
- Transboundary users: N/A
- Lake Argyle is Western Australia's largest and Australia's second largest freshwater artificial reservoir by volume (Wikipedia, 2016w).

Key water uses

Irrigation, hydropower.

Irrigation

Lake Argyle is one of two major reservoirs of the Ord River Irrigation Scheme. The irrigated area is approximately 12 500 ha.

Hydropower

The hydroelectric station of Lake Argyle supplies electricity to Kununurra, Wyndham and the Argyle Diamond Mine. It comprises two Francis turbines of 7.5 MW capacity each. The annual energy output of the dam is 220 GWh (Lake Argyle, 2016b).

Others

Lake Argyle is also used for fishery and recreation.

Goods and services provided

Irrigation, electricity, fishery, recreation.

Stakeholders

Government

- Commonwealth Government of Australia
- Government of Western Australia, including Department of Water, Western Australian Planning Commission and Environmental Protection Authority of Western Australia.

Primary users

- Farmers
- Fishers
- Downstream communities.

Others

- Pacific Hydro Pvt. Ltd.
- Tourists and tourism service providers
- Research institutes
- Ramsar organisation.

Brief history

The Australian Commissioner of Tropical Agriculture first proposed damming the Ord River more than 100 years ago. In 1941, Carlton Reach Research Station (Ord River Experimental Station) was set up to explore the possibilities of irrigation in the region. Due to positive results, a diversion dam – Kununurra Diversion Dam – was planned to irrigate the Ivanhoe plains. Construction on the diversion dam began in late 1960; it was commissioned in 1963. In 1967, grants were provided to construct the Ord River Dam. Construction started in 1969 by American Dravo Corporation and the dam was officially opened in 1972. In 1996, the spillway wall was raised by 6 m to double the dam's capacity (Lake Argyle, 2016a).

Business model for MPWI financing, including cost recovery

The Commonwealth Government of Australia financed the construction of the Ord River Dam for USD 22 million in 1967. The Ord River Cooperative (OIC) operates and manages water and drainage services to farms. According to OIC, the water tariffs are:

- OIAMC Asset Levy: USD 63.22/ha
- Fixed Levy: USD 165.00/ha
- Volumetric: USD 6.00/ML
- Pumping surcharge: USD 0.50 cents/ML.

Key challenges

- Lake Argyle remains Australia's most underused reservoir in the context of supply of irrigation water.
- A wide range of issues must be addressed around water allocation to expand uses of Lake Argyle for aquaculture, recreation and tourism.
- The full potential of goods and services in and around Lake Argyle has yet to be realised.

Positive externalities

- Switching from diesel power to hydroelectricity after commissioning of Lake Argyle has saved nearly 60 million litres/year of diesel fuel in East Kimberly.
- The new ecosystem developed with the filling of Lake Argyle resulted in the largest freshwater reservoir in Australia. It turned the lake into a unique ecosystem with a wide range of fish, bird, mammal and other species (Lake Argyle, 2016c).
- Lake Argyle facilitates research in weather and water quality, as well as freshwater crocodiles (Lake Argyle, 2016e).
- It is one of the most attractive tourism and recreational hot spots in Australia.
- The lake is recognised as an important wetland area under the Ramsar Convention; with Lake Kununurra, it forms the Lakes Argyle and Kununurra Ramsar site (Australian Government, Department of the Environment and Energy, 2016).

Negative externalities

- Lake Argyle remains Australia's most underused lake in the context of human activity.
- The ecosystem has been negatively affected.

Specific regulations

The management and regulation of the reservoir lie under the "Ord River Management Plan" of the Department of Water, Government of Western Australia. Under this plan, the water of the Ord River must be managed in the following ways:

- Protection of the riverine environment of the lower Ord River
- Hydroelectric power provisions at the Ord River Dam
- Hydroelectric power provisions at the Kununurra Diversion Dam
- Provisions for a fishway at the Kununurra Diversion Dam
- Sustainable diversion limit from Lake Kununurra to Tarrara Bar
- Sustainable diversion limit downstream of House Roof Hill (Government of Western Australia, 2006).

The spillway of Lake Argyle's Ord River Dam was raised by 6 m in 1994 to double the capacity of the lake, as well as to reduce the threat of sedimentation of the reservoir (Dixon and Palmer, 2010).

Future

State and federal governments of Australia have funded to expand the irrigation areas of the Ord River Irrigation scheme. Expansion is focused on increasing the irrigated farm areas of 12 500 ha to 45 000 ha with construction of the second main irrigation canal (Lake Argyle, 2016f).

The Western Australian government released USD 322.5 million for phase 2 of the Ord project in 2010. This phase involves building the essential infrastructure to enable the release of 13 400 ha of land for irrigated agriculture (Australian Government, 2016).

The Department of Planning of Western Australian Planning Commission has proposed to develop Lake Argyle as a special control area. This would require identifying and developing future opportunities in Lake Argyle. The main components of the proposal are expansion of tourist accommodation, and assessing the possibilities of aquaculture and recreation (Anon, 2016c).

6.15. Lake Mead (Hoover Dam), Colorado River Basin, United States of America

Owners, including asset ownership

United States Bureau of Reclamation.

Physical characteristics:

- Volume: 36 700 MCM
- Surface area: 581 km^2
- Residence time: 283.5%
- Total internal renewable water resources per capita: 8 758 m^3/inhabitant/year
- Climatic condition: Arid
- Transboundary users: N/A.

Lake Mead is the largest reservoir in the United States, measured by water storage capacity.

Key water uses

Irrigation, hydropower, flood and drought risk management.

Irrigation

Lake Mead provides storage for the annual runoff of the Colorado River. It provides water supply for irrigating over 400 000 ha of land in southern California, and southwest and central Arizona. These irrigated areas include Palo Verde Valley, Yuma Valley, Imperial Valley and Coachella Valley.

Hydropower

With 17 power generators, the maximum generation capacity of the hydroelectric station is 2 080 MW. The annual hydroelectricity generation of Hoover Dam varies – from the minimum of 2.648 TWh in 1956 to a maximum of 10.348 TWh in 1984. On average, the dam has generated 4.2 TWh/year for 1947-2008. In 2015, the dam generated 3.6 TWh (Wikipedia, 2016y).

Flood and drought risk management

The dam primarily prevents the yearly threat of flood damage to the fertile regions below the dam by controlling the water of the Colorado River (Power Authority, 2012).

Others

The lake provides water to about 20 million people in the states of Arizona, Nevada and California. The top of the dam forms the bridge to cross the Colorado River. There are two lanes (on Route 93) for automobile traffic across the top of the dam.

Goods and services provided

Flood control (primary concern), irrigation, electricity, drinking water, navigation.

Stakeholders

Government

- Federal government and federal agencies
- State agencies.

Primary users

- Households
- Farmers
- Industries
- Native American communities.

Others

- Tourists
- Research institutes.

Brief history

Since about 1900, the Black Canyon (where the dam is located) and nearby Boulder Canyon were investigated for their potential to support a dam that would control floods, provide irrigation water and produce hydroelectric power. In 1922, the Reclamation Service presented a report for construction of a dam on the Colorado River to control floods and generate electricity. The Congress of America finally authorised the project in 1928 with construction starting in 1931. The Hoover Dam was built during the Great Depression to help combat unemployment. Due to the scope of the project, a consortium called Six Companies, Inc. was created, and it won the bidding process. The difficult summer weather and lack of facilities near the site presented many challenges.

Both, the dam and the power plant were completed in 1936, two years ahead of schedule and USD 15 million under budget. The dam was handed over to the federal government on 1 March 1936.

Most of the water in the reservoir comes from snowmelt in the Colorado, Wyoming and Utah Rocky Mountains. Inflow to the reservoir is controlled by another reservoir built upstream – Glen Canyon Dam, which is required to release water to meet the demands of Lake Mead. The flow of the Colorado River is managed between seven US states that are part of the river basin. In recent years, the entire region has been facing reduced flow, leading to historic low levels in the reservoir (see Figure 6.4).

Figure 6.4. **Upstream of the Hoover dam, September 2016**

Source: © BRAATHEN Nils Axel, OECD.

Business model for MPWI financing, including cost recovery

The Bureau of Reclamation made the bid documents available at USD 5 per copy on 10 January 1931. As part of the contract, the government provided the materials, and the contractor prepared the site and built the dam. The dam was designed over ten years and, contractors were required to follow the detailed specifications. The bid was accompanied by a USD 2 million bid bond; the winner had to post a USD 5 million performance bond. There were penalties if construction went over the seven years of stipulated construction time. To oversee design and engineering aspects of the project, Congress assigned a board of consulting engineers in 1928 to advise the Bureau of Reclamation.

The construction of the dam cost USD 49 million in 1931. In 1934, Congress authorised a 50-year contract (i.e. from 1937 to 1987) to sell electricity. Selling power generated by the dam over the 50 years was intended to recover costs. This led to legislation that empowered the Interior Secretary to set the price of electricity over the 50-year period. This revenue also financed the multimillion-dollar yearly maintenance budget. The electricity was proposed to be divided among the Metropolitan Water District (36%), City of Los Angeles (13%), Southern California Edison Company (9%), and the states of Nevada and Arizona (18% each), with a total contract value of over USD 327 million. In 1984, Congress passed a new statute that set power allocations from the dam from 1987 to 2017.

Originally, the Los Angeles Department of Water and Power and Southern California Edison Co. ran the powerhouse. However, in 1987, the Bureau of Reclamation assumed control. In 2011, Congress extended contracts until 2067, after setting aside 5% of Hoover Dam's power for sale to Native American tribes, electric co-operatives and other entities.

Key challenges (faced in the past, at times of construction)

- States within the basin of Colorado River had litigation issues.
- The similar design to St. Francis Dam, which collapsed in 1928, raised concerns about design and engineering.
- It was difficult to support construction in the Black Canyon, a remote area with harsh climatic conditions. This created difficulties for housing, feeding and general care for the workers, as well as transportation and supply of equipment, water and electricity. Safety and health issues of construction workers were intensified by the extensive number of simultaneous operations.
- Due to uncertainty in the availability of buyers for the generated hydroelectric power, it was difficult to ensure profitability. It was also a challenge to determine the hydroelectric power tariff for the project to compete with other sources of electricity and attract potential buyers, while ensuring profitability for the government.
- Water and power need to be divided equitably between the seven basin states and other potential buyers.
- The unusual size of the project and other parameters made delivery of the project impossible for an individual construction company. The extremely high bid and performance bonds required of bidders by the government meant that few, if any, individual companies could qualify to bid. The USD 5 million performance bond was one of the main reasons that led to the establishment of Six Companies, Inc. (Kwak et al., 2014).
- Increasing demand combined with prolonged multi-year climatic drought has led to precipitously low reservoir levels in Lake Mead. This has led to the closing of tourist hot spots of Lake Mead.
- Reduced agricultural runoff due to the shrinkage of Lake Mead could threaten the Colorado River Delta (Jiang et al., 2015).

Positive externalities

- Construction of Hoover Dam employed 5 000 Americans suffering from the Great Depression (U.S. Department of the Interior, 2000).
- Lake Mead National Recreation Area provides over one-third of the economic and tourism value in the Colorado River Basin due to its proximity to the major metropolitan centre of Las Vegas. More than 125 small businesses depend on the recreation industry at Lake Mead and create 3 000 local jobs (Wikipedia, 2016z).
- Hoover Dam is a major tourist draw, attracting nearly a million people each year. Lake Mead provides many types of recreation to locals and visitors. Boating is the most popular. Additional activities include fishing, water skiing, swimming and sunbathing.

Negative externalities

- The changes in water flow due to construction and operation of the Hoover Dam have had a huge impact on the Colorado River Delta.
- The dam has been blamed for the decline of this estuarine ecosystem. For six years after construction of the dam, while Lake Mead filled, virtually no water reached the mouth of the river.

- The delta's estuary once had a freshwater-saltwater mixing zone stretching 40 miles (64 km) south of the river's mouth. It was turned into an inverse estuary where the level of salinity was higher close to the river's mouth.
- The Colorado River had experienced natural flooding before construction of the Hoover Dam. The dam eliminated this natural flooding, threatening many species that had adapted to its patterns, including both plants and animals.
- The construction of the dam devastated populations of native fish in the river downstream from the dam. Four species of fish native to the Colorado River, the Bonytail chub, Colorado pikeminnow, Humpback chub and Razorback sucker, are listed as endangered (SlideShare, 2010).
- After construction of the dam, the groundwater table deepened due to the lowering of Colorado riverbed.

Specific regulations

The 1922 "Colorado River Compact" is an agreement among the seven US states in the basin of the Colorado River in the American Southwest. It governs allocation of rights to the river's water. (Wikipedia, 2016x) As per the Compact, the entire basin is divided into two areas – the Upper Division (made up of Colorado, New Mexico, Utah and Wyoming) and the Lower Division (made up of Nevada, Arizona and California). Both areas have to supply equal amounts of water to the river based on rainfall patterns before the treaty. Since then, the weather pattern seems to be changing in the region. There has been persistent drought, leading to interim guidelines in 2007 for three conditions in Lake Mead – light shortage, heavy shortage and extreme shortage. These are based upon surface elevation of the lake.

In 2012, the International Boundary and Water Commission of the United States and Mexico signed Minute 319 to decide on how the water will be released to Mexico during surplus and drought years.

Future

Due to changing climate and lower flow in the river, the reservoir height is falling. Five wide-head turbines – designed to work efficiently with less flow – will go online in 2017. This will help lower the minimum power pool elevation from 1 050 feet to 950 feet (320 m to 290 m).

References

ADB (2015), *Regional Power Transmission Project (RRP TAJ 43150-02) – Summary Sector Assessment: Energy*, Manila.

Aladin, N.V. and I.S. Plotnikov (1993), *Large saline lakes of former USSR: a summary review*, Hydrobiologia, Vol. 267, pp. 1-12.

Albiac-Murillo, J. (2015), *Water Pricing Experiences and Innovations,* Springer International Publishing, pp. 1-12.

ANDRITZ Hydro (2013), *HYDROMATRIX® Jebel Aulia – Sudan*, https://www.andritz.com/resource/blob/31694/d1218a9d68692d3f2522bb9be2b9f831/hy-hydromatrix-jebel-aulia-en-data.pdf (accessed 18 August 2016).

Anon (2016a), *Gariep Dam*, wis.orasecom.org/content/study/UNDP-GEF/InfrastructureCatalogue/Documents/Reservoirs/Gariep%20Dam.pdf (accessed 16 August 2016).

Anon (2016b), *The problem of water in Southern Africa and in particular the management of water in South Africa*, www.agroparistech.fr/IMG/pdf/Lustenberger_en_sr.pdf (accessed 16 August 2016).

Anon (2016c), *Lake Argyle Development Node*, www.planning.wa.gov.au/dop_pub_pdf/kwadssec8.pdf (accessed 11 August 2016).

Antipova, E. et al. (2002), *Optimization of Syr Darya water and energy uses*, Water International, 27(4), pp. 504-516.

Attarzadeh, M.R. and J. Vatanfada (2011), *Iran and Turkmenistan: Lessons Learned from Transboundary Water Cooperation*, www.unece.org/fileadmin/DAM/env/documents/2011/wat/Int._Conference/presentations/Session_5/1_Iran_Attarzadeh_Iran_Turkmenistan__lessons_learned_from_transboundary_water_cooperation_2011-dec.pdf (accessed 22 August 2016).

Australian Government (2016), *Lakes Argyle and Kununurra – Australian Ramsar Site No. 3*, Department of the Environment and Energy, www.environment.gov.au/cgi-bin/wetlands/ramsardetails.pl?refcode=32 (accessed 11 August 2016).

Australian Government (2016), *Expansion of the Ord River irrigation scheme*, Department of Industry, Innovation and Science, http://northernaustralia.gov.au/page/water/expansion-ord-river-irrigation-scheme (accessed 12 August 2016).

Awulachew, S.B. (2012), *The Nile River Basin: water, agriculture, governance and livelihoods,* Routledge.

Baboo, B. (1991), *State policies and people's response: Lessons from Hirakud Dam*, Economic and Political Weekly, pp. 2373-2379.

Barbour, K.M. (1959), *Irrigation in the Sudan: its growth, distribution and potential extension. Transactions and Papers*, In: Transactions and Papers *(Institute of British Geographers),* No. 26, pp.243-263.

CA&CC Press AB (2016), *Tajikistan's Hydropower Resources*, www.ca-c.org/journal/2003/journal_eng/cac-03/20.peteng.shtml (accessed 21 July 2016).

CAWATER (2016a), *Library*, www.cawater-info.net/library/ca_e.htm (accessed 26 August 2016).

CAWATER (2016b), *Water resources use*, www.cawater-info.net/bk/water_land_resources_use/english/docs/water_res_use.html (accessed 26 August 2016).

Central Water Commission (2012), *National Register of Large Dams: A compilation of state-wise large dams in India by Central Water Commission.*

Chave, P.A. (2001), *The EU water framework directive: an introduction*, IWA publishing.

Choudhury, P., J. Sandbhor and P. Satapathy (2012), *Floods, fields and factories: Towards resolving conflicts around the Hirakud Dam*, Odisha State Resource Centre.

Degeorges, A. and B.K. Reilly (2006), *Dams and large scale irrigation on the Senegal River: impacts on man and the environment*, In: International Journal of Environmental Studies, 63(5), pp.633-644.

Dixon, R.N.M. and D.W. Palmer (2010), *Lake Argyle sedimentation – 2006 survey*, Department of Water, Salinity and Land Use Impacts Series, Report No. 42.

Dumont, H. J. (2009), *The Nile – Origin, environments, limnology and human use*, Springer, New York, USA.

EBRD (2009), *Turkmenistan Country Profile*, www.ebrd.com/downloads/legal/irc/countries/turkmenistan.pdf (accessed 22 August 2016).

EFSD (2015), *Toktogul HPP Rehabilitation in Kyrgyz Republic*, https://efsd.eabr.org/en/projects/toktogul-hpp-rehabilitation-in-kyrgyz-republic/ (accessed 18 December 2017).

EzEldin, M.A.M. et al. (2008), *Engineering Geological Assessment of Sandstone Rock from Jebel Aulia New Hydroelectric Power Plant Site, Jebel Aulia Dam, Sudan*, In: Journal of Engineering and Applied Sciences, Vol. 3, No. 3, pp.109-117.

Faisal, J. (2012), *Comparison of Electricity Supply and Tariff Rates in South Asian Countries, Energy Forum of Sri-Lanka*, www.efsl.lk/reports/electricity_supply_south_asian_countries.pdf (accessed 19 August 2016).

FAO (1994), *Reservoir Fisheries Resources of India: Orissa*, Food and Agriculture Organisation, Rome.

Fraval, P. et al. (2002), *The quest for integrated and sustainable water management in the Senegal River Valley*, In: 5th Inter-Regional Conference on Environment and Water, ENVIROWATER, pp. 5-8.

Frida-Tolonen, F. (2014), *Promotion and Development of Tourism in Cameroon*, Laurea University of Applied Sciences.

FuniQ (2016), *Lake Tisza*, http://en.funiq.hu/816-lake-tisza (accessed 19 August 2016).

Gakusi, A., L. Delponte and S. Houetohossou (2015), *Fostering Regional Integration in Africa: Lessons from Manantali Energy Project (Mauritania, Mali & Senegal)*, In: JSS, 03(03), pp. 91-102.

GENI (2016), *Energy Overview of Hungary*, www.geni.org/globalenergy/library/national_energy_grid/hungary/EnergyOverviewofHungary.shtml (accessed 19 August 2016).

GIBB & SMEC (2000), *Aral sea basin program, water & environmental management project component C: dam safety and reservoir management, Kayrakkum dam, safety assessment report*, www.cawater-info.net/bk/dam-safety/files/kayrakkum-dam-en.pdf, Tashkent.

Glantz, M.H. (2005), *Water, climate, and development issues in the Amu Darya Basin.* Mitigation and Adaptation Strategies for Global Change, 10(1), pp. 23-50.

Government of Republic of Kazakhstan (2016), Постановление Правительства Республики Казахстан от 8 апреля 2016 года № 200 Об утверждении Генеральной схемы комплексного использования и охраны водных ресурсов [Decree of the Government of Kazakhstan as of 8 April 2016, No. 200 "On approval of the General Scheme for complex use and protection of water resources"], Government of Republic of Kazakhstan.

Government of Western Australia (2006), *Ord River Water Management Plan*, Water Resource Allocation Planning Series Report No. 15, Department of Water.

Gupta, R.P., G. Kawadia and S. Attari (2007), *Chambal Valley Development Project: Unequal Distribution of Gains*, Economic and Political Weekly, pp. 397-402.

Gupta, R.P. and G. Kawadia (2003), *Rainfall and Run-Off: Changing Trends in Gandhi Sagar Dam*, Economic and Political Weekly, pp. 3457-3459.

Himanshu, T. (2010), *Why Gandhisagar is an Oxymoron? The strong case for reducing the FRL of the Chambal Dam*, W.G.S., Dams, Rivers & People, http://sandrp.in/dams/The_strong_case_for_reducing_Water_Level_of_Gandhi_Sagar_Dam_Dec_2010.pdf (accessed 18 May 2017).

HydroWorld (2016), *Kyrgyzstan seeks electrical components, instrumentation to refurbish 1200-MW Toktogul hydro project*, www.hydroworld.com/articles/2015/05/kyrgyzstan-seeks-electrical-components-instrumentation-to-refurbish-1-200-mw-toktogul-hydro-project.html (accessed 23 August 2016).

HydroWorld (2015), *ILF to service USD169 million modernization at Tajikistan's 126-MW Kayrakkum hydroelectric project*, www.hydroworld.com/articles/2015/12/ilf-to-service-us-169-million-modernization-at-tajikistan-s-126-mw-kayrakkum-hydroelectric-project.html (accessed 25 August 2016).

Inogate (2015), *A review of energy tariffs in inogate partner countries*, www.inogate.org/documents/A_Review_of_Energy_Tariffs_in_INOGATE_Partner_Countries.pdf (accessed 23 August 2016).

International Rivers Africa Program (2016), *A Case Study on the Manantali Dam Project (Mali, Mauritania, Senegal)*, www.internationalrivers.org/resources/a-case-study-on-the-manantali-dam-project-mali-mauritania-senegal-2011 (accessed 9 August 2016).

International Rivers Africa Program (2010), *African Dams Briefing 2010*, Berkeley, USA.

Jain, S.K., P.K. Agarwal and V.P. Singh (2007), *Hydrology and water resources of India*, Springer, Dordrecht.

Jiang, N. et al. (2015), *The Bathtub Ring. Shrinking Lake Mead: Impacts on Water Supply, Hydropower, Recreation and the Environment*. Getches-Wilkinson Center for Natural Resources, Energy, and the Environment, University of Colorado Law School, Colorado.

Kaya, I. (1998), *The Euphrates-Tigris basin: An overview and opportunities for cooperation under international law*, Arid Lands Newsletter 44.

Keshavarz, A. et al. (2005), *Water Allocation and Pricing in Agriculture of Iran*, https://www.nap.edu/read/11241/chapter/12 *(accessed 18 December 2017).*

Khaitov, A.H. et al. (2013), *Fisheries and Aquaculture in the Tajikistan: review and policy framework*, FAO Fisheries and Aquaculture Circular No. 1030/3, Ankara.

Kraak, E. (2012), *Central Asia's dam debacle*, https://www.chinadialogue.net/article/4790-Central-Asia-s-dam-debacle (accessed 14 July 2016).

Kwak, Y. et al. (2014), *What can we learn from the Hoover Dam project that influenced modern project management?*, International Journal of Project Management, 32(2), pp. 256-264.

Lake Argyle (2016a), *East Kimberley History*, www.lakeargyle.com/explore-and-learn/east-kimberley-history/(accessed 12 August 2016).

Lake Argyle (2016b), *Hydroelectricity at Lake Argyle, East Kimberley*, www.lakeargyle.com/explore-and-learn/hydroelectricity/ (accessed 12 August 2016).

Lake Argyle (2016c), *Lake Argyle Ecosystem*, www.lakeargyle.com/explore-and-learn/ecosystem/ (accessed 12 August 2016).

Lake Argyle (2016d), *Ord River Irrigation Scheme*, www.lakeargyle.com/explore-and-learn/ord-river-irrigation-scheme/ (accessed 12 August 2016).

Lake Argyle (2016e), *Scientific Freshwater Crocodile Research*, www.lakeargyle.com/explore-and-learn/scientific-research/ (accessed 12 August 2016).

Lake Argyle (2016f), *Ord Irrigation Scheme*, www.lakeargyle.com/wp-content/uploads/2013/04/Lake-Argyle-Ord-Irrigation-Scheme.pdf (accessed 12 August 2016).

Lovas, A. (2013), *A Közép-Tisza-vidéki Vízügyi Igazgatóság kiemelt fejlesztési tervei az Európai Unió 2014-2020*, Szolnok.

Mail Online (2016), *Bomb us if you dare: ISIS militants holed up in Syria's largest dam.* www.dailymail.co.uk/news/article-3412205/Bomb-dare-Senior-ISIS-militants-holed-Syria-s-largest-dam-high-value-prisoners-knowing-air-strikes-unleash-apocalyptic-flood.html (accessed 16 August 2016).

Mandsaur (2016), *Places of Tourist Interest*, www.mandsaur.nic.in/tour.htm#GANDHI SAGAR DAM (accessed 23 August 2016).

MEHR (2016), *Iran, Turkmenistan "hail extension of bilateral trade"*, https://en.mehrnews.com/news/116393/Iran-Turkmenistan-hail-extension-of-bilateral-trade (accessed 18 December 2017).

Mills, D.E. (2015), *Dividing the Nile: Egypt's Economic Nationalists in the Sudan 1918-56*, Oxford University Press.

Ministry of Irrigation and Water Management of the Republic of Tajikistan, UNDP Office in the Republic of Tajikistan and Executive Committee of the International Fund for saving the Aral Sea (2006), *Water sector development strategy in Tajikistan*, Dushanbe.

Nairizi, S. (2016), *Doosti Dam on shared river of Harirood: A Friendship Bridge Between Iran and Turkmenistan*, www.ais.unwater.org/ais/pluginfile.php/90/course/section/124/3.%20Nairizi%20Iran%20-Doossti%20DAM-Power%20point1.ppt (accessed 22 August 2016).

Nayak, A.K. (2010), *Big dams and protests in India: A study of Hirakud dam*, Economic and Political Weekly, pp. 69-73.

Olaore, A. and G. Aja (2014), *The Impact of Flooding on the Social Determinants of Health in Nigeria: A Case for North-South Institutional Collaboration to Address Climate Issues*, In: Developing Country Studies, 4(22), pp. 6-12.

Olsson, O. et al. (2008), *The role of the Amu Darya dams and reservoirs in future water supply in the Amu Darya basin*, In: Qi J. and K.T. Evered (eds.), *Environmental Problems of Central Asia and their Economic, Social and Security Impacts. NATO Science for Peace and Security Series C: Environmental Security*, pp. 277-292, Springer, Dordrecht.

Petr, T. (2003), *Fisheries in irrigation systems of arid Asia,* FAO Fisheries Technical Paper No. 430, Rome.

Power Authority (2012), *Hoover Dam*, www.powerauthority.org/about-us/history-of-hoover/ (accessed 12 August 2016).

Propastin, P. (2012), *Problems of Water Resources Management in the Drainage Basin of Lake Balkhash with Respect to Political Development*, Climate Change and the Sustainable Use of Water Resources, pp. 449-461, Springer.

Rahi, K.A. and T. Halihan (2010), *Changes in the salinity of the Euphrates River system in Iraq. Regional Environmental Change*, 10(1), pp. 27-35.

Rátz, T. and I. Vizi (2004), *The impacts of global climate change on water resources and tourism: the responses of Lake Balaton and Lake Tisza*, www.academia.edu/2660159/The_impacts_of_global_climate_change_on_water_resources_and_tourism_the_responses_of_Lake_Balaton_and_Lake_Tisza (accessed 18 December 2017).

Roggeri, H. (2013), *Tropical freshwater wetlands: a guide to current knowledge and sustainable management*, Springer Science & Business Media.

Schmidt, R. et al. (2006), *Bankable feasibility Study for Rogun HEP Stage 1 construction completion in Tajikistan*, In: Berga, L. et al. (eds.), *Dams and Reservoirs, Societies and Environment in the 21st Century*, pp. 405-413, London.

Schmidt-Soltau, D. (2004), *Water energy nexus in Central Asia: improving regional cooperation in the Syr Darya Basin*, World Bank, Washington, DC.

Shahin, M. (2006), *Hydrology and water resources of Africa*, Springer.

Simpson, D.W. and S.K. Negmatullaev (1981), *Induced seismicity at Nurek reservoir, Tadjikistan, USSR*, Bulletin of the Seismological Society of America, 71(5), pp. 1561-1586.

Sinaei, V. (2011), *Hydropolitics and Human Security: Water Cooperation in Relations between Iran, Afghanistan and Turkmenistan*, Iranian Review of Foreign Affairs, Vol. 2, No. 3, pp. 111-134.

SlideShare (2010), *Hoover Dam and the negative effects on environment*, www.slideshare.net/Lengkengs/hoover-dam-and-the-negative-effects-on-environment-4204612 (accessed 12 August 2016).

Soboleva, O.V. and U.A. Mamadaliev (1976), *The influence of the Nurek Reservoir on local earthquake activity*, Engineering Geology, 10(2-4), pp. 293-305.

SOGEM (2016), *Barrage de Manantali*, www.sogem-omvs.org/barrage.html (accessed 9 August 2016).

Srivastava, H.N. et al. (1995), *Reservoir associated characteristics using deterministic chaos in Aswan, Nurek and Koyna reservoirs*, Pure and Applied Geophysics, Vol. 145, pp. 209-2017.

Starodubtsev, V.M. and V.A. Bogdanets (2011), *New deltas formation in large water reservoirs*, https://www.researchgate.net/publication/265786125_NEW_DELTAS_FORMATION_IN_LARGE_WATER_RESERVOIRS.

Sudan Vision Daily.

Szabó, K. et al. (2005), *Epiphytic diatoms of the Tisza River, Kisköre Reservoir and some oxbows of the Tisza River after the cyanide and heavy metal pollution in 2000*, Acta Botanica Croatica, 64(1), pp.1-46.

Teasley, R.L. and D.C. McKinney (2011), *Calculating the benefits of transboundary river basin cooperation: Syr Darya Basin*, Journal of Water Resources Planning and Management, 137(6), pp. 481-490.

Tilmant, A. (2007), *Impacts of the south-eastern Anatolia Project in Turkey on the performance of the Tabqa dam and hydropower plant in Syria*, Proceedings of Symposium HS3006 at IUGG2007, Perugia, July 2007, Vol. 315, p. 1.

Times of India (2012), *Winged guests start arriving at Hirakud reservoir*, http://timesofindia.indiatimes.com/home/environment/flora-fauna/Winged-guests-start-arriving-at-Hirakud-reservoir/articleshow/17570321.cms (accessed 27 August 2016).

Tisza-tavi Okocentrum (2016), *Ecocentre*, www.tiszataviokocentrum.hu/en/(accessed 19 August 2016).

Toro, S.M. (1997), *Post-Construction Effects of the Cameroonian Lagdo Dam on the River Benue*, In: Water and Environment Journal, 11(2), pp.109-113.

UN Water (2013), *Kyrgyzstan: UN-Water Country Brief*, www.unwater.org/publications/un-water-country-briefs-kyrgyzstan/.

U.S. Department of the Interior (2000), *Hoover Dam, Learning Packet*, https://www.usbr.gov/lc/hooverdam/educate/hoovered.pdf (accessed 12 August 2016).

Vatanfada, J. and C. Mesgari (2014), *Doosti Dam Progress on Water Cooperation*, www.unece.org/fileadmin/DAM/env/documents/2014/WAT/04April_9-10_Geneva/presentations/2.3_Doosti_Dam-Iran_Vatanfada_Hajimesgari.pdf (accessed 23 August 2016).

Votrin, V. (2003), *Transboundary water disputes in Central Asia: using indicators of water conflict in identifying water conflict potential*, Vrije Universiteit Brussel, Master's Thesis.

Wikipedia (2016a), *Gariep Dam*, https://en.wikipedia.org/wiki/Gariep_Dam (accessed 16 August 2016).

Wikipedia (2016b), *Jebel Aulia Dam*, https://en.wikipedia.org/wiki/Jebel_Aulia_Dam (accessed 18 August 2016).

Wikipedia (2016c), *John Watson Gibson*, https://en.wikipedia.org/wiki/John_Watson_Gibson (accessed 18 August 2016).

Wikipedia (2016d), *Lagdo Reservoir*, https://en.wikipedia.org/wiki/Lagdo_Reservoir (accessed 19 August 2016).

Wikipedia (2016e), *Manantali Dam*, https://en.wikipedia.org/wiki/Manantali_Dam (accessed 9 August 2016).

Wikipedia (2016f), *Lake Assad*, https://en.wikipedia.org/wiki/Lake_Assad (accessed 16 August 2016).

Wikipedia (2016g), *Tabqa Dam*, https://en.wikipedia.org/wiki/Tabqa_Dam#Project_history (accessed 16 August 2016).

Wikipedia (2016h), *Water resources management in Syria*, https://en.wikipedia.org/wiki/Water_resources_management_in_Syria (accessed 16 August 2016).

Wikipedia (2016i), *Water supply and sanitation in Iraq*, https://en.wikipedia.org/wiki/Water_supply_and_sanitation_in_Iraq (accessed 16 August 2016).

Wikipedia (2016j), *Ganghi Sagar Dam*, https://en.wikipedia.org/wiki/Gandhi_Sagar_Dam (accessed 23 August 2016).

Wikipedia (2016k), *Climate of India*, https://en.wikipedia.org/wiki/Climate_of_India (accessed 23 August 2016).

Wikipedia (2016l), *Gandhi Sagar Sanctuary*, https://en.wikipedia.org/wiki/Gandhi_Sagar_Sanctuary (accessed 23 August 2016).

Wikipedia (2016m), *Hirakud Dam*, https://en.wikipedia.org/wiki/Hirakud_Dam (accessed 27 August 2016).

Wikipedia (2016n), *Iran-Turkmenistan Friendship Dam*, https://en.wikipedia.org/wiki/Iran-Turkmenistan_Friendship_Dam (accessed 22 August 2016).

Wikipedia (2016o), *Electricity pricing*, https://en.wikipedia.org/wiki/Electricity_pricing (accessed 22 August 2016).

Wikipedia (2016p), *Kapchagay Reservoir*, https://en.wikipedia.org/wiki/Kapchagay_Reservoir (accessed 24 August 2016).

Wikipedia (2016q), *Lake Balkhash*, https://ru.wikipedia.org/wiki/Балхаш# (accessed 24 August 2016).

Wikipedia (2016r), *Kayrakkum Reservoir*, https://en.wikipedia.org/wiki/Kayrakkum_Reservoir (accessed 25 August 2016).

Wikipedia (2016s), *Nurek Dam*, https://en.wikipedia.org/wiki/Nurek_Dam (accessed 27 August 2016).

Wikipedia (2016t), *Toktogul Dam*, https://en.wikipedia.org/wiki/Toktogul_Dam (accessed 26 August 2016).

Wikipedia (2016u), *Lake Tisza*, https://en.wikipedia.org/wiki/Lake_Tisza (accessed 19 Aug. 2016).

Wikipedia (2016v), *Tisza Dam*, https://en.wikipedia.org/wiki/Tisza_Dam (accessed 19 August 2016).

Wikipedia (2016w), *Lake Argyle*, https://en.wikipedia.org/wiki/Lake_Argyle (accessed 11 August 2016).

Wikipedia (2016x), *Colorado River Compact*, https://en.wikipedia.org/wiki/Colorado_River_Compact (accessed 12 August 2016).

Wikipedia (2016y), *Hoover Dam*, https://en.wikipedia.org/wiki/Hoover_Dam (accessed 12 August 2016).

Wikipedia (2016z), *Lake Mead*, https://en.wikipedia.org/wiki/Lake_Mead (accessed 12 August 2016).

World Commission on Dams (2000a), *Dams and Development: A New Framework for Decision-making: the Report of the World Commission on Dams,* Earthscan Publications Ltd, London, www.internationalrivers.org/sites/default/files/attached-files/world_commission_on_dams_final_report.pdf.

World Commission on Dams (2000b), *Orange River Development Project, South Africa – Final Report*, Cape Town.

Chapter 7

Conclusions and lessons learned

This chapter presents four main conclusions from the case studies. It describes how benefits from reservoirs typically transcend expectations for the dams, and how initial funds from construction come from the state or bilateral loans. It also looks at the nature of the business model, as well as positive and negative externalities. The chapter ends with challenges associated with dams and reservoirs, particularly for developing countries.

Benefits of reservoirs transcend expectations of dams

The dams are usually built with one or two objectives, but the benefits from the reservoirs typically transcend expectations. All the reservoirs studied in the case studies were built to generate hydropower and provide water for irrigation (except Tisza in Hungary). Some (such as Hirakud in India, Hoover in the United States and Jabel Aulia in Sudan) were built predominantly to control floods. However, they also help generate hydropower and supply water for irrigation. The reservoirs built by these dams became source of fisheries for the local community. Most also provide recreational services. Some reservoirs (such as Kapchagay Reservoir in Kazakhstan, Tisza in Hungary and Mead Reservoir in the United States) become great tourist destinations, boosting the local economy. Many reservoirs develop their own ecosystems and are home to multiple species of migratory birds or support diverse wildlife (e.g. Hirakud in India, Kayrakkum in Tajikistan and Argyle). Some reservoirs (such as Lake Assad in Syria and Doosti at the Iran-Turkmenistan border) provide necessary water to neighbouring urban centres. Consequently, stakeholders for these reservoirs go beyond government, which are the investors and managers, to include energy producers, farmers, fishers, households and tourists.

Initial funds for construction come from the state or loans

Initial capital for construction of these reservoirs/dams was either provided by their respective government or mobilised through loans. The government of the Soviet Union funded and built all the dams in Eastern Europe, Caucasus and Central Asia (EECCA) region. Other countries provided investments and loans to build most of the dams in developing countries. The Chinese government funded Lagdo Dam in Cameroon, for example. About 16 donors funded the Manantali Dam in Mali. These donors included German and French development co-operation, the African Development Bank, the World Bank, the European Investment Bank, Canada, Saudi Arabia, Kuwait and the United Nations Development Programme. Jebel Aulia in Sudan was built with funding from Egypt. The Soviet Union provided a loan to build Assad Dam in Syria. Some hydropower plants are operated by private organisations including multinational companies (such as a South African company operating hydropower in Manantali Dam in Mali). In terms of cost recovery, there are clear structures defined for collecting tariffs for hydropower generations. However, these are not always defined for water provided for irrigation.

The business model does not account for all benefits

Reservoirs generate other economic benefits such as fisheries and tourism, but they are not typically included in initial studies. Indeed, none of these other economic benefits are considered for cost recovery, revealing weaknesses in the business model.

Externalities are multiple and can be positive or negative, depending on context

Positive externalities include development of fisheries, tourism, biodiversity enrichment, hotspot for migratory birds and flood protection. The negative externalities include displacement of existing communities, flooding of historic and archaeological sites, siltation and spread of disease.

Some externalities from the reservoirs could be either negative or positive, depending on the context. Although the dams distort the natural flow of river and negatively impact fisheries downstream, they provide new fisheries opportunities in the reservoir. Although less flow leads to modifications of ecosystems downstream, reservoirs create new ecosystems around them. The reservoirs help control floods downstream, but sometimes the sudden release of water and lack of communication leads to floods and loss of both life and property downstream. Some studies show fewer seismic activities due to the presence of reservoirs (Kayrakkum Reservoir) whereas other studies show the opposite (Nurek Reservoir).

Some reservoirs are models of good transboundary co-operation. For example, Doosti Reservoir along the Iran and Turkmenistan border; or Manantali Dam in Mali jointly owned by Mali, Mauritania, and Senegal through their shares in the tripartite Manantali Energy Management Company.

Conversely, transboundary conflict has arisen due to construction and operations of Lagdo and Assad reservoirs in Cameroon and Syria respectively.

Reservoirs in EECCA countries that were part of the Soviet Union, initially built to provide irrigation water to downstream farmers, were managed by a central authority. After disintegration of the Soviet Union, the upstream countries, although water-rich were short of energy. Hence, operations of their reservoirs shifted from irrigation to hydropower generation. This has created some conflicts with downstream countries, which are managed by multilateral agreements between the concerned EECCA countries.

Challenges

There are many challenges during the life cycle of a multi-purpose water infrastructure (MPWI). In the initial stage, social conflicts arise due to displacement of communities, which would be flooded. Developing countries also have issues with raising adequate capital for construction of an MPWI. Management of reservoirs depends upon the inflow of water, which further depends upon management of the upstream watershed. This sometimes create conflict between upstream stakeholders and MPWI management. Water release schedule for hydropower generation and irrigation often do not match, which creates conflicts between stakeholders in their respective sectors. In some instances, sudden releases of water and miscommunication lead to floods downstream of the MPWI.

Typically, there are no clear mechanisms for cost recovery for operations and management of multi-purpose dams. This partly contributes to lack of proper management of these infrastructures.

Further reading

Abbink, K., L.C. Moller and S. O'Hara (2005), *The Syr Darya River conflict: an experimental case study*, www.igier.unibocconi.it/files/documents/events/SyrDarya.pdf (accessed 18 December 2017).

Adams, A. (2000), *The Senegal River: Flood management and the future of the valley.* International Institute for Environment and Development, Issue Paper/Drylands Program (93).

AFRODAD (2011), *Mapping Chinese development assistance in Africa: An analysis of the experiences of Cameroon*, African Forum and Network on Debt and Development, Harare, https://www.africaportal.org/publications/mapping-chinese-development-assistance-in-africa-an-analysis-of-the-experiences-of-ethiopia/.

allAfrica.com (2016), *Sudan: Rabak – "Largest Power Station in Sudan, Empty Hospital"*, http://allafrica.com/stories/201602090303.html.

Anon (2016), *Lake Argyle Development Node*, www.planning.wa.gov.au/dop_pub_pdf/kwadssec8.pdf (accessed 11 August 2016).

Branche, E. (2015), *Multipurpose Water Uses of Hydropower Reservoirs*, EDF-World Water Council, Marseille.

Cabestan, J.-P. (2015), *China-Cameroon relations: Fortunes and limits of an old political complicity*, South African Journal of International Affairs, Routledge, http://dx.doi.org/10.1080/10220461.2015.1014930.

CAREC (2011), Бассейновый План Интегрированного Управления Водными Ресурсами и Водосбережения Арало-Сырдарьинского Водохозяйственного Бассейна [Basin Plan for Integrated Water Resources Management and Conservation of the Aral-Syr Darya Basin], CAREC, Kyzylorda.

Committee on Water Resources (2015), Схема вариантов водоотведения в катастрофические по водности многоводные годы избыточных расходов в пески КЫЗЫЛКУМ [Various Water Management Schemes in case of Surplus Water in Kyzylkum], Committee on Water Resources, Government of Kazakhstan. R.

Ellender, B.R., O.L.F. Weyl and H. Winker (2009), *Who uses the fishery resources in South Africa's largest impoundment? Characterising subsistence and recreational fishing sectors on Lake Gariep*, Water SA, 35(5), pp. 677-682.

FAO (2016), *AQUASTAT – FAO's Information System on Water and Agriculture*, www.fao.org/nr/water/aquastat/countries_regions/tjk/index.stm, Rome.

FAO (1994), *Status of fish stocks and fisheries of thirteen medium-sized African reservoirs: Cameroon*, Food and Agriculture Organisation, Rome, www.fao.org/docrep/005/v4110e/V4110E02.htm (accessed 19 August 2016).

GRanD Database (2016). www.gwsp.org/products/grand-database.html.

Hale, J. and D. Morgan (2010), *Ecological Character Description for the Lakes Argyle and Kununurra Ramsar Site*, Report to the Department of Sustainability, Environment, Water, Population and Communities, Canberra.

Heyns, P. (2003), *Water-resources management in Southern Africa*, http://collections.unu.edu/eserv/UNU:2428/nLib9280810774.pdf#page=16 (accessed 16 August 2016), In: Nakayama, M., International waters in Southern Africa, United Nations University, pp. 5-37.

Hopper, B. (2005), *Integrated River Basin Governance. Learning from International Experience*, IWA Publishing, London, Seattle.

Inan, Y. (2000), *The law of international water courses and the Middle East*, J. Intl. Aff., 5, p. 2.

Keshavarz, A. et al. (2005), *Water Conversation, Reuse, and Recycling*, Washington, DC: The National Academics Press, pp. 153-280.

Ministry of Environmental Protection of the People's Republic of China and CWR (2016), *Water-nomics of the Yangtze River Economic Belt*, China Water Risk, Hong Kong.

Mozafari M., E. Raeisi and M. Zare (2012), *Water leakage paths in the Doosti Dam, Turkmenistan and Iran*, Environmental Earth Science No. 65, pp. 103-117.

Normatov, I. (2003), *The water balance and the solution of water problems in the Central Asian region*, International Association of Hydrological Sciences Publication 286, pp. 300-314.

OECD (2015), *OECD Principles on Water Governance,* OECD, Paris, https://www.oecd.org/cfe/regional-policy/OECD-Principles-on-Water-Governance-brochure.pdf.

OECD EAP Task Force (2013), *Improving the Use of Economic Instruments for Water Resource Management in Kyrgyzstan: The Case of Lake Issyk-Kul Basin*, OECD Publishing, Paris.

https://www.oecd.org/env/outreach/2013_Kyrgyz%20report%20on%20Eis%20for%20WRM%20Eng%20Web.pdf.

Ord Irrigation Cooperative Ltd, www.ordirrigation.com.au/.

President of the Republic of Kazakhstan (2016), План нации – Путь к казахстанской мечте [The Plan of the Nation – The Way to the Kazakh Dream], www.akorda.kz/ru/events/akorda_news/press_conferences/statya-glavy-gosudarstva-plan-nacii-put-k-kazahstanskoi-mechte.

President of the Republic of Kazakhstan (2014), "State Program for Water Resources Management", approved by Presidential Decree #786, 4 April 2014.

Regional Center for Renewable Energy and Energy Efficiency (2016), *Latest Electricity Price Schemes in RCREEE Member States*, www.rcreee.org/content/latest-electricity-price-schemes-rcreee-member-states.

Sadoff, E.W. et al. (2016), *Securing Water, Sustaining Growth: Report of the GWP/OECD Task Force on Water Security and Sustainable Growth*, University of Oxford.

Sen, S. (2015), Top 3 Methods of Irrigation (With Diagram), webpage, www.yourarticlelibrary.com/irrigation/top-3-methods-of-irrigation-with-diagram/60659/.

Starodubtsev, V.M. and S.R.Truskavetskiy (2011), *Desertification processes in the Ili River delta under anthropogenic pressure*, Water Resources, 38(2), pp. 253-256.

Annex A

Glossary

English

Terms	Definitions
Consumer surplus	Consumer surplus is the extra benefit consumers gain when they pay less than they were prepared to pay.
Economic welfare	Economic welfare is economic well-being expressed in terms of the sum of consumer and producer surplus.
Market agents	In this report, the key groups of agents are considered producers, consumers and the state (public authorities); when analysing impact on other sectors, the energy sector is also considered.
Producer surplus	Producer surplus is the extra benefit for producers when they sell their product at a price greater than the unit costs of production.

Source: Own elaboration based on Economics Online (www.economicsonline.co.uk/) and own definition of "market agents".

Russian

Термины	Определение
Излишек производителей	Излишек производителей – это такая дополнительная выгода для производителей, когда цена, по которой они фактически продают свой товар, выше издержек его производства.
Потребительский излишек (дополнительная выгода для потребителя)	Потребительский излишек – это такая дополнительная выгода для потребителей, когда цена, которую они фактически уплачивают, ниже цены, которую они готовы были платить.
Участники рынка	В данном отчете: это производители, потребители и государство (публичная власть); при анализе влияния на другие сектора сюда добавляется также сектор энергетики
Экономическое благосостояние	Экономическое благосостояние – это благосостояние, выражаемое как сумма Излишка производителей и Потребительского излишка.

Источник: Собственная разработка, основываясь на Economics Online (www.economicsonline.co.uk/) и собственное определение «участников рынка».

Annex B

Institutions visited and persons met

Name	Position	Contact details
Astana		
Yerdos Kulzhanbekov Tursynbekovic	Senior Expert, Committee on Water Resources, Ministry of Agriculture	e.kulzhanbekov@msh.gov.kz
Arman Orazovic Ajmenbetov	Deputy General Secretary, Committee on Water Resources	8 (717) 2374598 Ao_lawyer@bk.ru
Nazgul Saduova	Head of Unit, Committee of Housing and Communal Utilities, Ministry of National Economics	8 (717) 274 18 15 Na.saduova@economy.gov.kz 742775@mail.ru
Saule Zhadrina	Senior Expert, Committee of Housing and Communal Utilities, Ministry of National Economics	-
South Kazakhstan Region		
Meirbek Egenov	Director, Kazvodkhoz, South Kazakhstan Branch	ugvodhoz@mail.ru
Tolkyn Balpikov	Deputy Director, Kazvodkhoz, South Kazakhstan Branch	8 (701) 742 25 28
Karl Albertovic Anzelm	Head, South Kazakhstan, Hydrogeological Agency, Committee on Water Resources	8 (701) 376 79 23 8 (705) 437 43 21 Ggmeak55@mail.ru
Meirzhan Yusupbekovic Esanbekov	Deputy Head, South Kazakhstan, Hydrogeological Agency, Committee on Water Resources	8 (778) 660 09 73 Meyr_1984@mail.ru
Abdukhamid Urazkeldiev	Chief Engineer, Yuzhvodstroi	urazkeldiev@mail.ru
Polatbaj Zumataevic Tastanov	Deputy Head, Department of Agriculture, *Akimat* of South Kazakhstan *region*	8 (725) 251 21 70 Dsh_uk@mail.ru

Annex C

Mission, April 2016

This annex contains information about the mission in April 2016 to Astana, Shymkent and Shardara cities to launch the data collection.

18 April 2016, Astana
Committee on Water Resources of the Ministry of Agriculture

19 April 2016, Shymkent

- Water Committee agencies
  - Local *Kazvodkhoz* (water resources and infrastructure management in South Kazakhstan)
  - Aral-Syr Darya Basin Inspection
  - South Kazakhstan Hydrogeology and Melioration
- *Akimat* of South Kazakhstan region
  - Department of Agriculture
  - Energy and Utilities Department

20 April 2016, Shardara

- Shardara Reservoir
- Kyzylkum Canal operation

Annex D

Expert workshop, September 2016

Purpose

This annex reports on conclusions and recommendations from Day 1 of the expert workshop in Astana, Kazakhstan, on 15-16 September 2016. Day One was devoted to the project titled "Strengthening the role of multi-purpose water infrastructure". The agenda for Day 1 is provided as well.

Conclusions

- Presentations and preliminary findings (refurbishment of Kyzylkum Canal, improved drainage, increased use of drip irrigation, renovation of the drinking water supply system and tariff reform in the Shardara MPWI) were well-founded, interesting and useful for investment planning. Several participants praised the use of actions, scenarios and storylines.
- It was noted – and very much welcomed – that the model developed and applied in the project will be made publicly available.
- The model may be applied in other MPWIs in Kazakhstan (and outside Kazakhstan as well).
- The model may be used to assess implications of various financing schemes for the government budget.
- Further use of the model may support implementation of State Program for Water Resources Management adopted in 2014. This programme, among other points, calls for construction of 29 new reservoirs in Kazakhstan.

Recommendations

- Use the project – and the model developed and applied in the project – for investment planning in Kazakhstan at national level, akimat level and reservoir or MPWI level.
  - Replicate the project in other reservoirs or MPWIs in Kazakstan, at first in Kapchagay Reservoir about 60 km north-east of Almaty.
- Disseminate the model properly to improve investment planning.
  - Make the model available at a user-friendly website that has a cockpit in which the user may make certain choices, that makes it possible to run the model without any particular software installed on the laptop and presents results in terms of selected standard tables and figures.
  - Train civil servants, researchers and PhD students in use of the model.

- Title the model WHAT-IF, which stands for **W**ater-**H**ydropower-**A**griculture **T**ool – **I**nvestments & **F**inancing (or Water-Hydropower-Agriculture Tool for Investments & Financing), highlighting how the model addresses the water-energy-food nexus.
- The government of Kazakhstan and international organisations should inform the Executive Committee of the International Fund for Saving the Aral Sea about the project and the WHAT-IF model.
  - The OECD was encouraged to apply the model in other countries in Central Asia, specifically for Toktogul Dam and Upper-Naryn cascade, both in the Kyrgyz Republic.

Agenda

The agenda for Day 1 at the expert workshop in Astana, Kazakhstan, on 15-16 September 2016:

Time	Session and presentations	Speakers
9:00-9:30	Registration of participants	
9:30-10:00	Opening session	
	Welcoming speech	Mr. Dauletiar Seitimbetov, Deputy Chairman, Water Resources Committee, Ministry of Agriculture of the RK
	OECD activities in Kazakhstan	Mr. Alexander Martoussevitch, OECD
	Tour de table: Introduction of participants	All participants
10:00-10:45	Methodological considerations, MPWI	
	Definitions, actions and schematic	Mr. Jesper Karup Pedersen, COWI
	Questions and answers	All participants Facilitation: Mr. Alexander Martoussevitch, OECD
10:45-11:30	Scenarios – Towards policy recommendations	
	Scenarios for MPWI in South Kazakhstan	Mr. Mikkel Kromann, COWI
	Policy discussion in two groups on possible policy recommendations regarding: • sectors and crops; • actions to be taken (in terms of investments in Shardara MPWI); • financing	All participants Facilitation: Mr. Alexander Martoussevitch, OECD, and Mr. Jesper Karup Pedersen, COWI
11:30-11:45	Coffee break	
11:45-12:00	Brief reporting from groups	Appointed Chairs of the two groups
12:00-13:00	Introduction to the model	
	Key features of the model developed – Structure, data requirements, user interface	Mr. Mikkel Kromann, COWI
	Questions and answers	All participants Facilitation: Mr. Jesper Karup Pedersen, COWI
13:00-14:00	Lunch	
14:00-15:45	International experience	
	MPWI in other countries – from selection criteria to 15 case studies	Mr. Aditya Sood, International Water Management Institute
	Discussion	All participants Facilitation: Mr. Alexander Martoussevitch, OECD, and Mr. Jesper Karup Pedersen, COWI
15:45-16:00	Coffee break	

Time	Session and presentations	Speakers
16:00-17:00	Closing session	
	Wrap-up, key messages emerging from discussions, Next steps	Mr. Mikkel Kromann, COWI, and Mr. Jesper Karup Pedersen, COWI
	Tour de table: Concluding remarks	All participants
	Closing statement	Mr. Alexander Martoussevitch, OECD

Annex E

WHAT-IF at a glance

This annex briefly describes the model which was developed and applied through this project.

Introduction

Overall purpose

The overall purpose of WHAT-IF is to facilitate a policy dialogue aimed at identifying and prioritising investments and governance actions – typically associated with a MPWI – in a certain river basin. It does so by assessing the impact of certain investments and governance actions on the economic value of water in the basin with a breakdown of expected net benefits by sectors (foremost, hydropower and agriculture), by key groups of economic agents (producers, consumers, and the state) and by provinces (or countries).

In other words, the overall purpose is to address and answer policy and research questions related to the investment portfolio (type, size and timing), governance and management actions (water pricing, land reform, energy market reform, etc.), such as:

- What if we want to maximise economic welfare in a river basin as a whole – What then are the priority investment projects associated with a MPWI?
- What if we want to maximise producers' surplus within a certain sector (e.g. hydropower) – How will this affect producers' surplus within other sector and consumer surplus?
- What if we want to maximise economic welfare in a river basin subject to certain hydrological constraints (e.g. certain minimal level of water table in a lake; or under certain water allocation rules in a dry year) – How will this affect the basin wide economic welfare, as well as the economic welfare by countries or regions, by sectors and also by producers' and consumers' surplus?
- What if we want to maximise economic welfare subject to certain budget constraints for CAPEX and OPEX?
- What if we renovate existing drainage systems?
- What if we invest more in new efficient irrigation technologies, such as drip irrigation?
- What if we focus our investments in irrigation on conveyance systems transporting water from the main intake structure to the field ditches?
- What if we enlarge existing reservoirs or construct a new main canal?

- What if we increase irrigation water tariffs, thereby enabling owners of irrigation system to maintain the infrastructure properly and make additional investments?
- What if we invest in increasing the power system by expanding HES capacity or building a new thermal power plant?
- What if we introduce an energy market reform?
- What if we assume a country wants to harm another country as much as possible – How big harm can it actually make?
- What if we introduce certain compensation schemes – May we then make all countries, regions and sectors better off?

Hence, WHAT-IF may be conceived as a pre-feasibility analysis tool capable of identifying and prioritising investments in MPWI in a river basin, while at the same time **paving the way for sound water allocation arrangements, compensation schemes and benefits sharing** across countries, regions and sectors, and the key groups of economic agents in a river basin.

Economic welfare in focus

Consequently, WHAT-IF is a multi-sector hydro-economic model that addresses the water-food-energy nexus, including trade-offs between water, food and energy. It does so from an economic welfare perspective insofar as the key objective is to maximise economic welfare under certain constraints such as fixed demand for nature. In other words, **it seeks to achieve as much economic value as possible out of water available under certain constraints**.

Scenarios and storylines

WHAT-IF facilitates the construction and analysis of scenarios and storylines developed based on identified actions (i.e. investments and/or governance actions) and established success criteria.[1] For a certain river basin there will, as a rule, be 5-10 scenarios and 2-3 storylines; the number of identified actions may be 15-20.

- A scenario consists of a set of specific assumptions regarding selected actions. A very simple scenario will contain one and only one action, which is compared with a *no action* scenario (business-as-usual, BaU). In some cases, it can be attractive that scenarios contain multiple actions e.g. in the case where two actions are expected to affect each other. With two actions, the scenario should enable both actions. However, it would still be interesting to compare with the two scenarios containing only each single action, as well as the *no action* scenario. The time horizon of a scenario must be decided.
- A storyline is simply a group of inter-related scenarios. Each storyline aims to tell a specific story, highlighting certain developments, changes and impacts. The order of scenarios is of utmost importance to the storyline.
- The scenarios and storylines can be simulated in the model and compiled into a result spreadsheet. This sheet contains the storylines, which shows how the indicators develop with the introduction of various combinations of actions.

In sum, synergies and interactions between various actions and impacts of these may be presented in a comprehensive way. Changes in economic welfare, employment, agricultural output, energy production, etc. can easily be traced.

Five steps: WHAT-IF has five steps as illustrated in Figure E.1. Participation of key stakeholders in all steps is required for a successful project.

Figure E.1. **Steps in using WHAT-IF**

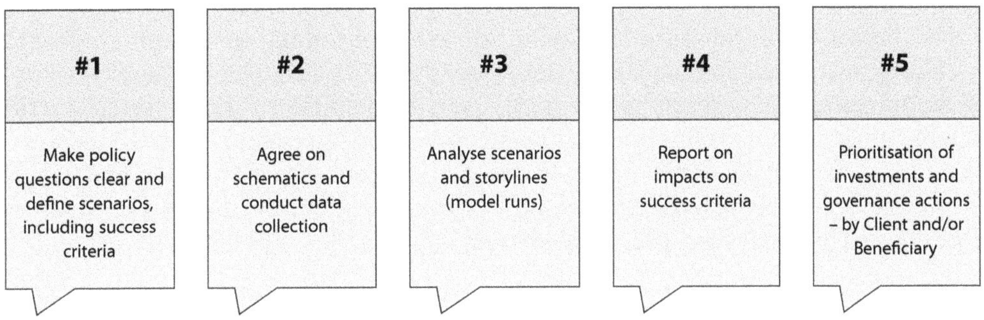

Source: Own elaboration by COWI.

Brief overview

Objective function

WHAT-IF calculates economic welfare as the sum of consumer and producer surplus under a Marshallian demand function. The model's objective function is to maximise this economic welfare.

Partial equilibrium model

The model can be labelled as a partial equilibrium model with a sophisticated description of hydrology and agricultural and energy production.

Model decision variables

It is a bottom-up technical/economical optimisation model, which simulates the decisions of various stakeholders in a river basin. Broadly speaking, there are three types of model decision variables:

- **Land use and crop choices:** The farmers must decide which crops to plant on which irrigated areas.
- **Reservoir management**: Monthly discharges must be decided to balance the need for irrigation water with the need for hydropower.
- **Irrigation choices:** The crops planted must be irrigated with whatever water there is available (under certain constraints or water allocation rules), possibly less than their optimal evapotranspiration, leading to reduced crop yields or contracted total area of irrigated land planted and harvested.

Model principles

The optimisation happens subject to a number of constraints (e.g. related to water scarcity or certain water allocation rules), which mimics real world limitations in physical responses. For instance, crop production is a function of land and water used, hydropower produced depends on the water level in the reservoir and water use priorities, the modelled flow of water must obey a mass balance restriction etc.

Key assumptions and sensitivity analyses

The limitations in physical responses are guided by **data** on hydrology, irrigated agriculture, energy, environment and other water uses. Selected data are supplemented by **scenario assumptions** chosen by the model user. These reflect various possible **actions** available to decision makers, e.g. investments in new infrastructure, changed taxation or operation of various facilities. Scenario assumptions can also be other circumstances, e.g. climate change. **Sensitivity analysis** with systematic variation to critical assumptions are performed by production additional scenarios.

Objective function and constraints

The objective function is enclosed in the model's welfare module. It counts the economic welfare of the various economic activities described by the model. To that end, it works with several constraints that limit the choices regarding decision variables (e.g. you cannot use more water than you have). The constraints are integrated into respective modules:

- **Hydrological mass balance module:** Flow of water through rivers and reservoirs respecting flow constraints of the user defined river system.
- **Agricultural module:** Farmers' optimisation of which crops to grow and how much water to apply given constraints on water and land use.
- **Energy module:** Energy production by hydropower stations, optimisation of the timing of reservoir discharge, and the economic value of the energy measured as the costs of the thermal energy production it replaces.

Each of these modules is implemented in a numerical optimisation model. As the optimisation problem is solved with respect to all constraints, the model will provide an integrated solution that considers all effects modelled.

Fiscal impacts

Fiscal impacts are accounted for separately. Accounting is made for all relevant taxes, subsidies (state support), as well as profits and losses in public and semi-public companies providing energy and water infrastructure services. Hence, it accounts for investments and change of service levels in MPWIs.

Overview

Figure E.2 illustrates the interactions of the various parts of the model.

Figure E.2. **Overview of the model**

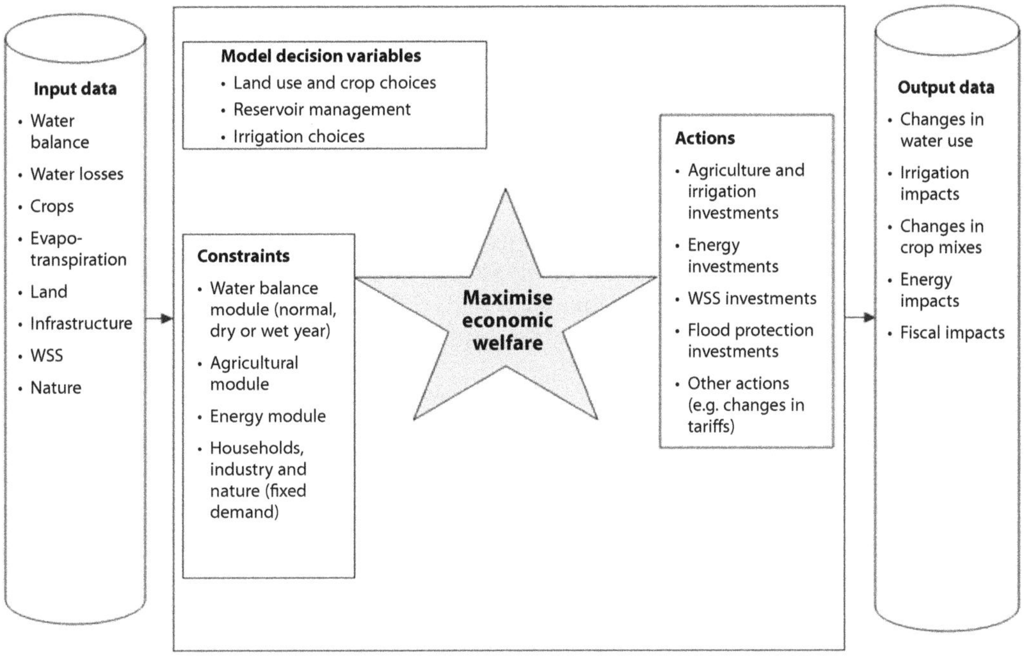

Source: Own elaboration by COWI.

Model design and operations

Capabilities and application

The model applies to the economic and financial analysis of an MPWI and its contribution to economy and to water, food and energy security. To that end, it weighs costs and benefits of water use in different sectors. It also simulates how actions, changed policies and new investments within one sector affect that sector, as well as other sectors and key groups of economic agents in each sector (producers, consumers and the state).

Bottom-up optimisation

As already mentioned, WHAT-IF is a bottom-up optimisation model accounting for carefully selected technical and economic and financial details within agriculture, hydrology and energy.

Adaptability

Furthermore, the model user has a high degree of control. Among other things, the user can count agricultural surplus and leave out energy sector surplus. Such a scenario would illustrate what happens when energy is not considered. Conversely, agricultural surplus can be ignored and only energy sector surplus could be optimised. Such a scenario would show the effects of ignoring agriculture in reservoir discharge decisions. It is also possible to assign different weights (a proxy for priorities) to agriculture and energy, creating various mixes for consideration.

Computing requirements

The model will run well on any modern standard personal computer. On a Pentium i3, for example, the model will solve typically within 10-60 seconds, depending on problem size and other technical considerations. Faster equipment will speed up the process. For modern computers, memory requirements are negligible (below 50-100MB RAM).

Data needs

Compared to hydrological models, this model relies on a relatively sparse data set. A river might be split into only a few sections (e.g. five). Agriculture is represented by agricultural planning zones (e.g. around five) with a limited number of crops (e.g. five-ten). Water flows are accounted monthly for only a few representative years (e.g. "dry", "normal" and "wet").

Plug-and-play capability

The model will generally run out-of-the box, provided the user has a working version of the numerical simulation software tool GAMS installed. Also, MS Excel and MS Access installations are required. The model is provided as a zip-file and can be placed anywhere on the user's computer.

User interface

Input data

The model input data are entered on an MS Excel spreadsheet containing 10-15 tables depending on delineation and scope of the model. Typically, each table has 10-15 rows and 10-15 columns (i.e. tables with input data are quite observable and manageable). Typically, an external consultant will initially fill out these tables, but subsequently any model user can inspect and change them.

Scenario assumptions

Additionally, scenario assumptions are entered on another MS Excel spreadsheet that also contains 10-15 tables with additional assumptions. These sheets typically contain rather simple information, such as economic and financial rates of return, assumed sensitivities for various prices, user financing, investment policies, reservoir operation behaviour, etc.

Assumptions organised as "policies"

All the assumptions are organised in "policies". These could be baseline and alternative policies for investments in canals, reservoirs, irrigation equipment, hydroelectric stations, etc. Or they could be policy on water-use priorities in (super-)dry years, translated into respective allocation rules, etc.

Scenarios combine policies

The user defines scenarios as combinations of various policies. Scenarios can be defined using a graphical user interface in the MS Excel sheet. The interface contains various drop-down menus to select policy, as well as various buttons for running simulations, and creating, copying and deleting scenarios.

Summarised and thematic result sheets

The results are presented in a third spreadsheet. The main findings are summarised in an overview fact sheet containing a few tables and figures showing the most important results. Additionally, around ten thematic sheets present various themes, such as water flows, energy production, agriculture and reservoirs, in more detail.

Scenarios presented in storyline

In the result spreadsheet, the scenarios are presented in so-called storylines as described in Chapter 1.

Model result as indicators

The storylines are used for all indicators presenting model results. Indicators could be: change in economic welfare, energy and agricultural production, water use and water efficiency, for example. Because of the storyline concept, it is also straightforward to compare developments in different indicators alongside implementation of different policies in the storylines.

Accessibility

Important consideration

Methodology, calculations and data should be accessible and reproducible for any interested party. This will hopefully enhance participation of both key and minor stakeholders, during and after project implementation. In this way, it will enhance understanding of the analysis and its results. To achieve this effect, the model, its input data, assumptions and model results should be as freely accessible as possible.

Key users

In Kazakhstan, envisaged key users are Ministry of Agriculture, Committee of Water Resources (CWR) and the operator of all state-owned hydro-technical structures (*Kazvodkhoz*), other ministries, universities and research institutes.

Open source model ownership

The model consists of the input, scenario and result spreadsheet, as well as around 15 plain text files containing the GAMS code for the model. All these files are provided on an Open Source basis using GNU General Public License (GPL) version 3.0.[2]

No restrictions on use, modification or redistribution…

Any author of model code or modification owns his/her own contribution. However, no restrictions can be placed on use, modification and distribution of either model or modifications. Modifications must also be distributed under the GNU GPL 3.0 licence. This will ensure the model in any version remains Open Source, and that no party can restrict its use, modification and redistribution.

... but changes can be kept private

Modifications need not be published and distributed. The licence permits someone to keep his/her modifications private. However, if the model or modifications are distributed, the distributor cannot restrict the receivers' use, modification or re-distribution of modifications. Once changes to the model are distributed to other parties, they are also to be considered Open Source.

Data ownership

Most data in the model[3] are likely to be owned by various government agencies and other parties. Since the model is not useful without data, used data need to be distributed to stakeholders and other interested parties to promote accessibility. Data owners must grant permission to distribute the data alongside with the model.

Public domain data

In many cases, data are in the public domain (e.g. on a website). In this case, the data can be freely redistributed alongside with the model. Typically, this involves quoting the website address, and indicating any changes to the data. The data providers will typically have some sort of redistribution policy, to which users must comply.

Private data

In other cases, the best available data may be owned by organisations that either sell the data for profit or cannot share the data for other reasons. If data owners do not provide permission to freely redistribute the data, other paths must be sought. Redistribution may be permissible if data are aggregated or transformed in other ways. If permission for redistribution is impossible, the data simply cannot be used in this specific project without jeopardising its accessibility. In this case, it is preferable to use own assumptions based on the best freely available data.

Assumption of ownership

The assumptions are part of the work delivered by the consultant to the client. As such, the client owns the work. To further accessibility of the analyses, the client can choose to distribute the assumptions (i.e. the scenario spreadsheet data) in the public domain, with a Creative Commons licence,[4] or similar.

Result of ownership

As with assumptions, results (i.e. data inside the result spreadsheet) are also part of the works delivered from the project team to the client. Since results can be calculated by using the model, input data and assumptions, results do not need to be in the public domain or similar venue for maximum accessibility. If results are not placed in the public domain, results data can simply be relicensed with no restrictions on redistribution. However, they would have restrictions on modification and quoting, e.g. a Creative Commons licence with a "No-derivative" clause.

Other administrative issues

Initial and operational costs

The model itself has no initial or operational costs. As Open Source, it is provided free of charge. The same goes for the selected dataset and assumptions, which are to be provided under permissive and cost-free licence terms.

Licence costs

The main part of the model is coded in the GAMS numerical programming and optimisation language. The data and results are kept in MS Access and MS Excel. To run simulations with the model, the user will need a licence for the GAMS system, as well as for MS Excel and MS Access. The GAMS licence costs USD 3 200 for a base system and USD 3 200 for an appropriate solver (the non-linear solvers CONOPT, MINOS5 and IPOPT have previously been confirmed to work with the model). The GAMS licence is perpetual, but as a point of departure it is attached to a specific person. Costs for MS Excel and MS Access may vary depending on the user's country.

Server location and costs

Previous experiences have shown it is possible to place a version of the model on a server connected to the Internet. Users can create and run scenarios on this server, and download the result spreadsheets (this option is not included in the current project on the Shardara MPWI).

Notes

1. See also Chapter 2.
2. www.gnu.org/licenses/gpl-3.0.html.
3. Using various formatting, the spreadsheets clearly mark the delineation – or scope of intellectual property rights (IPR) – between the model (which also includes the input, scenario and output spreadsheets) and its data and assumptions. Generally, "formulas" are considered as "model", while "raw numbers" are considered as "data". The model spreadsheets also include meta information tables for describing data IPR.
4. https://creativecommons.org/licenses/.

Annex F

Data

This annex provides an overview of the data collected during the project.

1. Water mass balance

Hydrology specialists from Aral-Syr Darya Basin Inspection have agreed to select the following years for project analysis:

- 2010 – Dry year
- 2012 – Normal year
- 2015 – Wet year.

Annual water balance data (including seepage and evaporation, environmental flows) were provided for the river sections (under Aral-Syr Darya Basin Inspection):

- Middle Syr Darya (from Kokbulak hydropost to Shardara Reservoir)
- Shardara Reservoir water mass balance
- Lower Syr Darya South Kazakhstan section (from Shardara Reservoir to Koktobe hydropost)
- Lower Syr Darya Kyzylorda section (from Koktobe hydropost to North Aral Sea). No more detailed split by Kyzylorda River sections was provided.

As advised by the Basin Inspection and the Committee of Water Resources under the Ministry of Agriculture, there is no available record of the monthly data for water mass balance.

Retrospective monthly data for the period of 1970s, 1980s and 1990s are available. But it is difficult to extrapolate the years with similar hydrological conditions due to significant change in land use and ageing infrastructure.

Data on monthly releases from Shardara Reservoir have been obtained.

2. Schematic

The schematics in Chapter 3 were compiled based on specific river sections received from the Basin Inspection and *Kazgiprovodkhoz* Institute, and consultations with selected experts.

3. Land use

Information on land use (for the specified hydrological years) in South Kazakhstan region was summarised by the South Kazakhstan Hydrogeology and Melioration Expedition (reports to CWR). This included land-use data derived from water supply analysis and data from the Department of Agriculture in the *Akimat* of South Kazakhstan region. The data detail land use by crops in the agricultural zones defined in Chapter 3. They also provide information on water use by agricultural zone and by main crop.

Information on land use in Kyzylorda region is given for rayons. Therefore, it will need to be aggregated by agricultural zones indicated in Chapter 3. It also provides information about water use by crops.

4. Land quality

Thanks to the South Kazakhstan Hydrogeology and Melioration Expedition, solid data were obtained for the level of land salinisation, groundwater level and mineralisation in specific agricultural zones of the South Kazakhstan region.

For Kyzylorda region, data were obtained from *Kazvodkhoz* branch in Kyzylorda, including the level of land salinisation, groundwater level and mineralisation.

5. Crops

Crop productivity and irrigation norms data are available for every rayon in Kyzylorda region and for every agricultural zone in South Kazakhstan region. Actual yields information is not available. However, it can be calculated based on land use and productivity (yield information is also available in Stat.gov.kz, but not detailed to fit the project needs).

For South Kazakhstan region, crop prices and detailed production costs were provided; for Kyzylorda region, the additional request was made to the Committee of Water Resources.

6. Irrigation infrastructure

The general information on canal systems and collector-drainage systems was obtained from the South Kazakhstan Hydrogeology and Melioration Expedition under the CWR. Specific information was provided regarding the Kyzylkum Canal use. Data on the general condition (depreciation level) of some infrastructure elements were provided; however, no capital or operational expenditures were specified (these data have been requested; alternatively, the comparative review from the IDIP-2 feasibility study may be used to assess the situation). The available data include irrigation methods by area and efficiency associated with their use.

7. Water users

As mentioned above, the data on water consumption in each irrigation system of South Kazakhstan region are available for analysis; however, Kyzylorda region gives no specification by irrigation zone.

Fishery needs in total are specified as a separate component in water balance. However, more detailed (by agricultural zone) information per water intakes for fishery needs has been requested for Kyzylorda region.

Environmental needs in total are specified as a separate component in water balance. However, more detailed data on water intakes (by agricultural zone) for environmental needs have been requested for Kyzylorda region. Certain assumptions have been made following information on the availability of lakes due to drainage-collector systems.

Regarding water supply data for drinking purposes and industrial sector in South Kazakhstan region, most urban and rural settlements use groundwater. The relevant data request was made to Energy and Utilities Department within the *Akimat* of South Kazakhstan region, which is responsible for some rayons. These data would help complete the mapping of water supply sources and consumption (*Yuzhvodstroi* responsible for group water pipelines provided the data for six rayons).

ORGANISATION FOR ECONOMIC CO-OPERATION AND DEVELOPMENT

The OECD is a unique forum where governments work together to address the economic, social and environmental challenges of globalisation. The OECD is also at the forefront of efforts to understand and to help governments respond to new developments and concerns, such as corporate governance, the information economy and the challenges of an ageing population. The Organisation provides a setting where governments can compare policy experiences, seek answers to common problems, identify good practice and work to co-ordinate domestic and international policies.

The OECD member countries are: Australia, Austria, Belgium, Canada, Chile, the Czech Republic, Denmark, Estonia, Finland, France, Germany, Greece, Hungary, Iceland, Ireland, Israel, Italy, Japan, Korea, Latvia, Luxembourg, Mexico, the Netherlands, New Zealand, Norway, Poland, Portugal, the Slovak Republic, Slovenia, Spain, Sweden, Switzerland, Turkey, the United Kingdom and the United States. The European Union takes part in the work of the OECD.

OECD Publishing disseminates widely the results of the Organisation's statistics gathering and research on economic, social and environmental issues, as well as the conventions, guidelines and standards agreed by its members.

OECD PUBLISHING, 2, rue André-Pascal, 75775 PARIS CEDEX 16
(42 2018 02 1 P) ISBN 978-92-64-28961-1 – 2018

www.ingramcontent.com/pod-product-compliance
Ingram Content Group UK Ltd.
Pitfield, Milton Keynes, MK11 3LW, UK
UKHW051503290926
15471UKWH00008B/1386

9 789264 289611